MW01295735

Free At Last
How to Make the Gospel Work

Will Riddle

2nd Edition

Please contact the author at will@thegonetwork.net if you would like to reproduce this book or sections of the book for your own purposes. All personal correspondence will receive a reply.

Printed in the United States of America

First Edition: January 2010

Second Edition: January 2012

ISBN 1449913768
EAN 978-1449913762

2

Contents

Introduction.. 6

Accept Responsibility.................................13

    DEAL WITH THE ROOT CAUSE 14

    BUT IT WASN'T ME.......................................19

    THE END OF MYSTICISM...............................38

    GET REAL 50

    PRIDE...56

    DON'T BE A PUNCHING BAG........................62

    END VICTIM THINKING................................67

Choose God 77

    TAKE RESPONSIBILITY.................................78

    GOD OR ENTERTAINMENT?..........................83

    DIE TO YOURSELF 90

Accept God's Love....................................95

    THE LOVE OF GOD 96

    GRACE 103

    WORKS...108

    YOU MUST BELIEVE...................................112

    EXPERIENCE GOD 117

Repent.. 121

    WHAT IS REPENTANCE?.............................122

    HOW SIN WORKS 130

    BRING IT TO GOD.....................................138

    TAKE AUTHORITY 150

    TRANSFORMATION TAKES TIME 157

Acknowledgements

The new edition contains a more practical and comprehensive teaching on repentance. I believe this will make applying the message much easier. I have also revised and expanded several important chapters. There were a number of places where big ideas needed further development to really make them clear. My hope is that these changes together will mean a much more user-friendly book.

Special thanks for this new edition of the book go to
- Becca Gruber for proofreading (I take full responsibility for the errors that remain!)
- Brad Gruber for helping me refine the concept of repentance.
- My wife Jaime for her numerous reviews to make the teaching clear.
- Everyone who has taken the message of the book seriously and applied it to their own life. Working with each of you is what has helped me see what areas needed improvement.

Thank you always to Jesus for loving me.

Contact Us!

If you like the message of this book, we encourage you to bring our team out to your church or fellowship to host a *Go Narrow* conference. *Go Narrow* is a weekend experience which helps congregations apply the message of this book. These encounters can be dramatic catalysts of revival. The Go Network has other conferences and materials which are all built on the message of personal responsibility:

- **Go Deep**: Looking for a way to rekindle that special "God spark" in your congregation? Building on the teaching in Go Narrow, we take your people into realms of intimacy with God which will fuel and empower their Christian life.

- **Go Revolution:** Designed to move people from the pews to places of action in God's Kingdom. We lay out God's big plan, and then help them find their specific place of action in God's master plan.

- **Go Out:** An innovative approach to evangelism which moves beyond traditional strategies and to the heart level of reaching the lost. Combining wisdom and the power of the Spirit, Go Out will open a new flow of evangelism in your life.

- **Go Truth**: Decodes what is going on in contemporary culture and the stance every Christian must take. Go Truth is Biblical Worldview like you've never seen it done before – practical, contemporary and hard hitting.

We encourage you to learn more about us at http://thegonetwork.net You may also contact me personally at will@thegonetwork.net All personal correspondence will receive a reply.

Introduction

When I was younger, I struggled with what seemed like unshakable guilt. I felt isolated and lost, like I might drop into the pit of hell at any moment or do something horrible God would never forgive. I was in a ministry which gave me no hope or understanding, so in desperation I put a prayer request on a random ministry website. I was expecting someone to just lift my concern up before God on their own time, but instead the senior pastor called me directly. He spent an hour talking to me, hearing my concerns, and then he said to me words I'll never forget: "There is a great big light at the end of your tunnel." It struck me. For the first time I started to feel like my personal prison was going to have a happy ending, and I started to close that chapter in my life.

Maybe you feel there is no hope for you. You've been to the altar a hundred times. You've confessed your sins. You've called out-of-state ministries for help. Maybe you've taken a variety of medications, but nothing seems to work. Or even tried to kill yourself. Maybe you are not much of a church person at all but you're looking for an exit door to a dead-end life. Perhaps you're actually not doing too badly, but there is one area of your life where you feel you will just never get the victory. Regardless of how far gone you are, I want you to know there is a great big light at the end of your tunnel too. When you've come to the end of yourself, you've reached the beginning of God.

If this is you, you may have to fight for your freedom, but I promise you there is One in your corner who is bigger than any problem and ready to move heaven and earth to break you free. No one ever loved you as much as He loves you. He knows the number of hairs on your head and the deepest secrets of your heart. And He knows the way out.

Maybe you are not as bad off as I was a decade ago. Maybe you absolutely on fire, effective in ministry, and respected by other Christians—but you have hit a ceiling you can't break through. You are fasting regularly, healing the sick, and reaching the lost, but something is missing and you don't know what it is. That's exactly where one of my ministry partners was when I shared the principles of this book with him. As he allowed these things to seep in, his walk with God and relationships began to change. He started moving into deeper and deeper places with God, experiencing heavenly encounters with God on a regular basis, and better relationships with friends and family.

It doesn't matter whether you are on the bottom like I was or on the top like my friend was, the keys in this book – Biblical keys – are what it will take to go deeper. If you are the kind of person who has come to the place where you are desperate for more of God, desperate for truth, the principles in this book will work for you. You will go to a deeper place with God. These principles will work with anyone in any walk of life. You may be in a dire situation or you may be mature in your walk with God. We have worked with both and found the message to be universally applicable.

On the other hand, if you aren't really ready to deal with difficult areas in your life, this book will not work for you. You may get excited momentarily, but when it becomes difficult, you will quit and look for another method. If there were an easier method, I would offer it to you, but I assure you there isn't. In order to become who you want to be, there is no way to avoid confronting who you are. This is why Jesus' ministry style seems so confrontational to us. He went straight for the main issue in each person's life that had to be dealt with in order to be His disciple.

THE FREEDOM PROCESS

We started our ministry with recovering addicts. We were taking tough cases that others had already given up on: people who had failed out of multiple treatment programs, had multiple addictions, and generally very difficult lives. In this situation, we, like many Spirit-filled believers, placed an emphasis on demonic deliverance. People were coming to us complaining of demons so we thought we should cast them out. While many people would have spiritual experiences, cry, and be touched, the long term fruit eluded us. What was missing?

After encountering the same problems over and over, our thinking changed. Certainly we know from Scripture and experience that the demonic realm is real and we are commanded to drive out demons (Matt. 10:8). We began to realize, however, that the real battle was ultimately in separating the human soul from sin and unbelief. This is where the demonic realm has its power.

This takes us back to the Garden of Eden, where man first gave authority to Satan. A close examination shows not only the psychology of the Fall, but the process by which God restored them. Modeled on this pattern and God's fulfillment of that process through the gospel, we have developed a very simple process to help you get free. In fact, our entire message could be summed up by saying the principles of salvation are the same principles for the victorious life: repent and believe. In theological terms, justification and sanctification work by the same mechanism (Gal 3:3).

The process of getting right with God may be fairly simple, but because of the complexities of sin and the deceitfulness of the human heart, there are a thousand ways to misunderstand it. This book is designed to deal with the nuances and make crystal clear how to find the way out of your struggles. We want to cut out the complexity and get you back to the clear teaching of the New Testament. Our experience is that if you walk through the steps as we have outlined them, you can break free from any bondage hindering your life. In other words, the gospel works.

Getting right with God begins with *accepting responsibility*. We all have elaborate methods by which we avoid responsibility—either for the commission of the sin or the responsibility for getting out of it. Getting to the place where you accept that you are the one who sinned, and you are the one responsible for exiting it, is the first major key to escape.

Many people are terrified of this step not just because they have spent their entire lives avoiding responsibility, but because they think God wants them condemned. They hear in their ears the accusations of misguided preachers, stern parents, or others, and want to do every-

1. Accept Responsibility

thing possible to avoid taking responsibility for their sin. It may hurt a little bit to come clean with everything, but it is nothing compared with the joy you will experience once you are free of it all. Sin is like a splinter God wants to remove. If you will stop protecting it and let Him remove it, things will get a lot better! The first section of this book is designed to expose the ways people protect the splinter by avoiding responsibility. If you don't reveal it, God can't heal it.

Once you see your sin, you must decide *you would rather have God than sin*. This is the step of total surrender. It is the realiza-

2. Choose God Over Sin

tion that right standing with God is a pearl of infinite worth which you would gladly trade anything else in your life to have. Many people are aware of their sin but are convinced it is so much fun that they would rather have it than God. It's a crazy choice to decide you would rather have the short term pleasure of sin than eternity in heaven. However familiar your sin is, I promise it's not worth permanent separation from God.

Many people get stuck on this step because they have confused the decision to turn away from sin with absolute perfect holiness. They keep trying to be perfect enough to approach God, but this will never work. You simply cannot overcome the power of sin until you have the love and grace of God working from inside of you. Many people are trapped, trying to fix their

9

sin by themselves in order to please God. They have confused turning to God with perfection. As long as you are trying to perfect yourself, you are guaranteed to fail. What you need at this point is a desire to be free at any cost, and a willingness to do whatever God says to get free.

It is in the third step, however, of *experiencing God's love*, that the power of Christ really begins. In the Old Testament, the Israelites glimpsed the love of God, but only the prophets and priests had direct access and experience with God. With the coming of Christ, however, the Love of God broke through. God Himself died on the Cross because He loved you so much that He did not want you to be apart from Him. Many people have been taught that God loves or chooses only some, but the Cross is God's emphatic declaration that He loves all. Jesus even tells us that the

3. Accept God's Love

Father "causes his sun to rise on the evil and the good, and sends rain on the righteous and the unrighteous" (Matthew 5:45). God's love for you is constant no matter what you do. Even if you are refusing to turn from your sin and trying to send yourself to hell rather than join Him in heaven, His love is still toward you. It is when you bring your sin to the Cross, however, that you actually *experience* the power of that love toward you. As long as you are holding onto sin or unbelief, you are saying in your heart, "This is better than having a relationship with God." Once you make the decision to release your sin to God and embrace His love instead, powerful things happen.

God's love is the foundation of everything positive you can experience in your walk with Christ. Until you are deeply rooted in it, you will not be able to have any real faith, and will walk through an unhealthy cycle of ups and downs. Most people have heard about God's love, and many believe in it, but coming to fully understand the breadth and depth of God's love, and then experience it, is another matter.

The final step in the process is to repent. True repentance is built on the foundation of God's love. You turn from sin and to love and relationship with God. Many people do not want to sin anymore and know God loves them and has forgiven them, but they are still unable to break free. Why is this? It is because they have not discovered how to actually apply God's love to their problems. In the fourth and final section of the book, we will teach you how to do this.

4. Repent

It is important that you walk the steps through in order. If you try to turn from sin before you have fully accepted responsibility for it, you will be fooling yourself. If you try to receive God's love before turning from sin, you will simply end up baptizing your sin. If you try to apply God's love before you experience it, you will be frustrated that your faith never avails any results.

~Part 1~

Accept Responsibility

Deal With the Root Cause

It seems strange that when Jesus saw the blind men by the road side He asked them, "What do you want me do to for you?" (Matthew 20:32). He obviously knew they were blind and could have easily assumed that they wanted their sight, but He asked them anyway. Why? I believe He wanted to know if they really wanted to change. It may seem obvious to you that the blind man needs healing, but is that what he really wants? The two blind men could have easily asked Jesus for a copper coin or a better mat to sit on.

God does not force people to change. In fact, even if God did force you to change, it wouldn't be real change at all, because it would be coming from outside. Real change comes from inside. Only when someone wants to change from within can real change happen. You would be surprised how many people would rather have a copper coin than to have their blind eyes opened. They come seeking ministry for the symptoms of their problem, rather than the problem itself. Are you one of them?

People usually come seeking ministry because they are experiencing a negative symptom of a problem. Something in your life is not working the way it is supposed to – your marriage, your living situation, your personal life, your walk with God – and so you become open to change. When this happens, the pressing problem of the moment looms larger than anything else, but it is really just a symptom of problems at work deep in your heart. Jesus likened Himself to a doctor (Mat 9:12), but a good doctor does not merely treat symptoms. A good doctor identifies the root cause so that a real solution can be provided, not one that merely takes the edge off the symptoms and pain.

Many people who go to the doctor have some idea of what they think their problem is, but these assessments are often wrong because they do not have the tools and training to look beyond the symptoms. The doctor will examine you and run tests to determine what is going on inside the body and then they will prescribe a solution. It is much the same way with spiritual and emotional problems. It's easy to focus on the symptoms, but you need to have the courage to drill to the root of the issue with the guidance of the Holy Spirit and ministers who speak the truth.

This is so important because the, "heart is deceitful above all things" (Jer. 17:9). By nature every person is self-deceived, deceived by others, and ultimately by the father of lies, Satan himself. The Holy Spirit and those who speak the truth to you can help you clearly see the cause of the problems and address the real root cause. This process, however, is surprisingly difficult. Many people, even when confronted directly with the root cause of their problems, persist in ascribing it to something else. Why is that?

Remember what happened in the Garden of Eden after they sinned? They felt ashamed and sewed garments to cover themselves up (Gen 3:7). God had to come and remove those garments to get at the root of the problem, which meant exposure and confrontation – something quite uncomfortable. It is this sense of shame and discomfort which lies at the root of the difficulty that most people have in dealing with or even identifying the real cause. Of course if you can never diagnose the problem, then you can never fix it. The very beginning of freedom is to learn to reconnect the consequences you are experiencing back to their ultimate cause. It is only once you diagnose correctly that you can apply the correct medicine.

What are you coming to Jesus for? What do you want? Do you want your symptoms gone, or do you really want to be healed of what is causing the pain? Our experience is that it is the rare person who is more interested in lasting change than relief from symptoms. What

> What you want to be free from will determine the outcome of your search.

15

about you? If you want a better life, but you're not ready to surrender to God, it will not work. What you want to be free from will determine the ultimate outcome of your search.

FINDING THE ROOT

Fortunately, God set up the world in a way which helps you confront the real root cause. This is the function of "the law." By this I do not mean the Law of Moses specifically, but rather God's truth of sowing and reaping which we can see in our relationships, culture, civil law, and the very nature of your physical existence. The law works such that whenever you veer off from doing what is right, you encounter a series of roadblocks and warning signs which tell you something is wrong. If you steal from your friend, he is angry with you and you lose a friend. If you drink until you pass out, you wake up in a strange place with a massive hangover. If you drive recklessly, you incur a citation or get in an accident. If you pay heed to these warning signs and get back on the right road, you can avoid a disaster. But if not, you will continue to hurt yourself, the innocent, and those you should love. In a nutshell, the "law" is what teaches you that good results in good, and evil results in evil.

Sometimes people resist or skirt the law of sowing and reaping. They think the consequences are unfair. It's like a fire. If you stick your hand in a fire, it hurts. The pain teaches you not to stick your hand in a fire. Imagine if you did not associate pain and the fire together. You would never learn not to put your hand in fire. This seems simple in the physical world, but not so simple in your own behavior. You keep sticking your hands into the fire of life but never connect the pain with the fire. The negative consequences are there to teach you what not to do. It is easy to see with others, but for your own life it is much harder to connect pain to its source.

Take loneliness as an example. When someone is lonely they usually start to feel like the world has failed them. No one really understands you. No one is like you. No one appreciates the deep things of life. All of these thoughts lead to depression. This depression leads you to seek help. This may lead you to take medication. But what can the medication do for you? Can it fix the root of your depression? Can it heal your loneliness? No. Only when you address the reason why you were lonely in the first place can you exit depression for good. Instead of connecting depression to the choices you made, or the way you are, you start to think the world is aligned against you. Emotional pain is there to tell you something is wrong. Blotting it out can only make your life worse. What you must do instead is connect pain back to sin and remove it. Then the pain will stop.

God tells us the causes of pain in his Word, but many people are simply not interested in the answer. You have been unable to find the root cause because you simply do not want to know it. When you get close to knowing the real reason for the problem, you deny it in favor of a fantasy – a fantasy that will not reflect negatively on you and does not require you to change.

In the move *Untouchables*, good cop Elliot Ness is disappointed because he has tried to find Al Capone's illegal stash of alcohol but keeps coming up empty. Finally, he meets the streetwise cop Jimmy Malone who explains to him why no one has been able to catch Capone. "Everybody knows where the booze is. The problem isn't finding it. The problem is who wants to cross Capone?" The problems you face in life are not really that complicated. They are complicated because the answer that will solve the problem is the one you are not willing to hear. Until you are willing to "cross Capone" – your sin – you will not be able to break free.

Many people look for the solution to their problems like a mathematician looking for an alternative answer to 1+1. If you rule out the correct answer from the beginning, every other solution is going to fail. It's like a man whose car will not start, but does not dare check the gas gauge and blames it on "bad luck" instead. If you embrace a fantasy about yourself, you ensure you will never solve the problems in your life. The "car" of your life will never start. Because no one likes to look or feel bad, it is easier to avoid the connection between sin and its consequences.

Are you centering in on an answer that you prefer more than the one you know is true? You got all those parking tickets because the cops were "out to get you." You went bankrupt because of the "corrupt banking system." Your money never came through, your spouse victimized you, the moon was in the wrong phase. Until you connect the problem to the real cause, you are stuck. Even if you could do something about the phase of the moon, it wouldn't put more money in your bank account.

Some people might even help you along in your deception. Remember the story of the "Emperor's New Clothes?" The emperor wanted a garment that would make him look better than everyone else, and by function of his vanity, was easily tricked into purchasing an invisible new robe. Because of the emperor's power and his unwillingness to hear the truth, no one dared tell the emperor he was naked. Many people around you know when you are naked, but they won't speak up because they know you won't hear the truth. They will continue to tell you they love your spotless garments, all the while suffering from the results of your behavior.

Similarly, some people will try to help you by "rescuing" you every time you fall. Thinking they are helping you, what they are really doing is causing the law of sowing and reaping not to work. Instead of discovering the consequences for your own actions, you learn if things get really bad, someone will jump in and bail you out. As soon as you are bailed out, you continue right back down the same road you were on. You might feel fine but the people rescuing you are exasperated to the breaking point because they are the ones reaping the consequences of your actions. Yet the more reliable the rescuers are, the more likely you are to abuse them. You will intentionally put the consequences of your actions on someone else in order to avoid them.

While there may be multiple causes to problems in someone's life, the one problem people usually can't see and won't fix is the one they actually have the most control over – themselves. This book is about helping you see the real cause, fix it, and walk to freedom. But it will only work if you really want the truth.

But It Wasn't Me

The Bible says there is "nothing new under the sun" (Ecc. 1:9). This could hardly be truer in any area than personal responsibility. From the very first sin of the very first man and woman, the human strategy of avoiding responsibility has been basically consistent: blame. Blame takes place any time you look for an excuse for why you did something wrong. It is a cup-shifting game. I did something wrong, but I do not want to feel bad about it or look bad in front of others, so I need an excuse. I need a reason, I need a motive, I need someone or something else to be at fault. Some people who are in love with their sin just use excuses as a cover. They have no intention of changing even when they are exposed. Most of us, however, are actually blinded by a complex system of excuses.

IF GOD HAD ONLY…

Ironically and sadly, the first person to take the blame is the only One guaranteed not to have contributed to the problem in any way: God. Remember Adam? When God asked Adam why he sinned, the first thing Adam said was, "because of the woman **you** gave me." Eventually he got around to saying, "Oh yes, I did eat that fruit but if *you* hadn't set me up for failure by putting this crafty woman in the garden, I never would have done anything." If you are human, your blame scripts is pretty similar. You do not mind admitting you did something wrong, as long as someone else gets to be the real cause: "Yes, Mom, I broke the window, but it was my brother's idea."

Why do people blame God, though? The main reason is they have the wrong view of God's role in the world. If God is in absolute control of everything, then it would be logical to blame Him for whatever happened. If one thing is clear from the

Bible, however, it is that God's will is not always done. Think about the Lord's prayer. Here, Jesus tells us to pray that God's will would be done on earth as it is in heaven. You may have said this a thousand times, but think about what Jesus actually is saying: God's will is being done in heaven, but it is not being done in the earth so you have to pray for it.

In fact, the entire point of the Gospel is that God's will is not being done on the earth. Christ died to save sinners, and what is a sinner except someone who is not doing the will of God? Therefore asking "Why did God let this happen?" is a fundamentally wrong question. If you were in heaven where God's will is always done it would be a good question, but you are on earth where God's will is rarely done. Evil things happen here simply because God allows the earth to continue to exist. As long as there is a place where God allows His will not to be done, bad things will happen.

But then why doesn't He just force everything to be good? This is impossible. We see from the Bible that demons can be forced to obey God, but that does not make them good. Being good, by definition is something that happens by choice, not by force. Therefore, if God were to "force" the world to be good, most people would simply be destroyed, as they were in the days of Noah and Lot. And if God were to enforce perfect purity, God would have to remove you and me too. When you ask, "Why did God allow this to happen" you are simply asking why earth is not like heaven, and the answer is, "Because people are here."

God gives human beings free choices, and we use those choices to do wicked things. The fact that you can do evil things and God does not wipe you out means other people can do evil things and God does not wipe them out. Think about it. God has already destroyed the world once because of all of the evil on it (Gen. 7). He has promised not to do that again until the end of history.

So you were born sinful among sinful people. Thank God He sent His Son to arrest the endless cycle of sin and start something new. When the gospel of Christ reaches you, the power to be free and something new has arrived. Without God, without a

Savior, this would be impossible. In whatever situation you find yourself, God is sending the power of Christ to overcome and change. The Israelites tried for over a thousand years to break the cycle in their own strength, which led only to their own destruction. God sent His Son because He wanted to make a definitive halt to evil. When God has His way in the world, the evil will stop. When God has His way in your life, the pain will stop.

Many Christians do not realize they are blaming God for their situation. Elaborate and subtle theologies cover what is really going on at a heart level. These theologies put the problem on God instead of us. Some are fond of describing adversity as God "testing" them. The problem with this is that it makes God out to be the cause, rather than the solution to the problem. Look at the Lord's prayer for a moment. Jesus taught us to pray "Lead us NOT into temptation, but deliver us from evil." (Mat 6:13). If you believe God is testing you, then you believe the exact opposite of what Jesus taught you to pray. You believe God is tempting you to see if you can pass the test, and He is bringing evil to see if you can survive. I have good news for you: God wants the sin and evil out of your life!

I believe this is the same thing James is attacking when he says "Let no one say when he is tempted, 'I am tempted by God' " (Jas. 1:13). It is natural for you to believe God is somehow orchestrating the difficulty in your life to see if you can make it, and that's why James had to address it. God has not brought difficulty into your life to see if you can make it. Either you brought the evil or another person brought it, not God. If there is difficulty in your life, He wants you to overcome it.

Many people read Romans 8:28 to mean that God causes bad things in a person's life to bring about good results. When people charged Paul with doing "evil so that good may come" (Rom. 3:8), he considered this a slander. So why do we think it is not slanderous to say the same thing about God? A closer look at Romans 8:28 reveals that Paul is teaching how God can turn every bad thing that happens to us around for a good purpose. In other words, God can make lemonade when you have only lemons.

God is also able to bring victory from defeat, and beauty from ashes. That is what Jesus did at the Cross, and that is what He wants to do for you. He didn't bring the evil in your life. And aside from allowing the post-Flood world to exist with sinful people on it, He didn't even permit it. God has been against evil from the beginning, and He is still against it. In fact, He sent Jesus to die in order to put a stop to evil altogether. I find the death of His only Son to be a pretty emphatic declaration of His will on this subject. I can promise you that there will be no evil things happening in heaven to refine your character, so why do you think God is doing that to you now? If refinement through pain were God's method for growth, then instead of a heaven where there is no mourning or crying or pain (Rev. 21:4), we would expect these things to continue.

> God has been against evil from the beginning, and he is still against it.

A very similar explanation of the bad in someone's life is, "so I can minister to others in the same situation." This is not really an answer at all. If something bad is happening to you in order for you to minister to others, then why is it happening to the *other person?* So they can minister to someone else? And what about that someone else? Do all bad things happen so someone can minister to them? The logic is absurd. It sounds like sending out the paramedics to shoot some people so they can do CPR. Bad things happen because of sin, period.

Last but not least, is the belief that you are "waiting on the Lord" to fix the problem. Actually, He is waiting on you. When Jesus ascended to heaven, He commissioned His disciples to go into all the world and make disciples, and He promised them that He would be with them always. He said He would send them a Comforter who would empower them to fulfill this commission. In other words, He put it all in their hands. He said He would bind it in heaven if we bound it on earth, yet a lot of us are running around trying to bind things in heaven while doing nothing on earth. God does not ordain seasons of doing nothing. He desires either you being changed or you changing others – preferably both. The saddest thing about "waiting" is that by waiting for God to do something, you are likely to become highly frustrated and ultimately angry with God. It's a lot like the popular clip of two people trapped on a stopped, open escalator becoming burnt out waiting for someone to rescue them.

The common theme of all these theological excuses is in allowing Satan to exchange his character for God's. The devil has been highly successful at getting the church world to do this. Satan already blames God for everything, and that's his goal for you too. He wants you to see God as mean, punishing, unfeeling, and ultimately the cause of your problems. This leads you to accuse God and be alienated from Him.

This is exactly what happened to Job. People read the book of Job to mean that God brought suffering on Job, yet this is completely the opposite of what the book really teaches. Job spends the entire book accusing God of bringing the suffering and becomes angrier and angrier. After all, if God is the reason for your problems, you have no hope of ever fixing them. If Job had been correct, then God would have commended him at the end. Instead God gives him one of the most excoriating rebukes in all of Scripture. The beginning of the book shows who was clearly trying to destroy Job's life – Satan. Job had the wrong guy. And if you are blaming God, you do too. If you think God is mean, punishing, unconcerned, and causing your problems, you've got God confused with someone else – Satan. God cannot be your help, your deliverer, your rock, your redeemer, and every other wonderful thing spoken of in Scripture if He is also the source of the problem.

In fact, that is the name of the game, isn't it? Once, we worked with someone who was tortured by voices that began when he was involved in drugs and the occult. Whenever the oppression was really bad, he would feel angry with God. He felt angry because he believed God was required to do something on his behalf. But it was Satan who was making his life miserable, whom he invited through his own actions. Part of getting this person free was bringing him to a place where he knew at the deepest reflex of his heart that God was his only friend and hope, not the one to blame when the going gets rough. Anger with God is evidence of wrong beliefs about God. Those beliefs make it almost impossible to receive anything from God because faith is rooted in the belief that God is good and He absolutely will come through (Heb. 11:6).

Blaming God will lead you on a journey of hopelessness. When your only friend becomes your enemy you will become angry and lose all hope. Blaming God will lead you to accept your situation rather than fix it. Because you feel your freedom hinges on God fixing it, you are able to accept your sin and accept others sinning against you. Instead, you need to evaluate your options. You almost always have a choice. Stand up in faith and do not be afraid to make the choices which will lead you out of the wilderness.

I KNOW I DID IT BUT...

Stepping back to Adam, remember how in the same breath he blamed not only God but the woman. Things haven't changed much, have they? Although it is common to blame God in theology, in daily life it is much more common to blame another human being. Blaming other people is the most common way of avoiding responsibility, probably because you are surrounded by them and they're flawed too.

Some people are angry that others have not done enough to help them. They may not blame people for causing their problems, but they blame them for not solving them. They are upset that others have not sacrificed more time and money to deal with them. They feel a solution is owed to them by society or the church. They are oblivious to the sacrifices that others are making for them all the time. Because they are not taking responsibility for their own problems, they are completely blind to the ability to see the responsibility that others are taking for them. The same sacrifices they demand from others they would not even begin to understand, much less make, for those people. They are benefiting from an invisible welfare system around them created by the church, society, parents, friends, and others. It is your responsibility to get free. It is not your job to blame people because you are not free.

In relationships, the natural human tendency is to exaggerate what others have done wrong and minimize what you have done wrong. Something bad happens and you make a reflexive choice – "Do I accept responsibility or do I blame someone else?" Jesus addresses this perception problem by saying you must remove the log from your own eye before dealing with the other person's speck. I used to think this meant as long as I thought my problem was smaller than a log, I could correct the other person. Boy was I wrong! Jesus is really saying, "You think you only have a speck, but it's actually a log. You think your neighbor has a log, but it's a speck."

We exaggerate the problems of others in order to avoid dealing with our own issues. If you are any part of the problem at all, even just a minor part, then you have to deal with your part — not the other person. If you did some-

Whose problems seem to justify your own?

thing wrong in a conflict, then your focus needs to be on you, not on the other person. It doesn't matter what fraction of the problem was yours, or who instigated the conflict. Take inventory of your life for a minute. In what areas are you focused on what others are doing to you? Whose problems seem to justify your own? As long as you are looking at the sins of others, you will have an endless list of reasons for why you can't change.

It is hard for me to overstate this point. If I had to pick only one thing which traps people, this is it. When a marriage fails, for example, it is often because two people became experts in their spouse's problems instead of confronting their own. Since you are a sinner, you know all about the problems of others. You demand they fix them. You think their problems are an excuse for your behavior. Sure you contributed, but they are the real villain. You expect them to wink at your sin but you refuse to do so for them. It's easy to see why this is a dead end. Two people finding fault and neither showing mercy means dysfunction and pain.

Jesus tells a parable about this attitude in Matthew 18:23-35. A master forgave his servant of a huge debt, but instead of turning around and forgiving those who owed him money, the servant went around demanding everyone pay him back. Needless to say, the master was incensed. The servant's behavior seems so outrageous, yet this is exactly what we do in the area of blaming others. You have received forgiveness and mercy from God, but you refuse to turn around and give it to others. You expect others to be merciful with you, but then turn around and demand perfection out of them.

Being a Christian demands that you forgive others just as you have been forgiven. It demands that you show mercy just as you have been shown mercy. Instead of throwing accusations, you must begin by understanding that they are human just like you. This means in a conflict you have to check your own heart. It seems so simple and obvious to examine your own behavior and deal with it, but many people never do this at all, especially in a conflict. As soon as they are wronged, it becomes all about raking the other person over the coals until they get restitution. Until you learn to look with mercy and love on the failings of others, and apologize when you have done anything wrong at all, your relationships will be miserable. Until you are ok being the bad guy, not having to prove you are right or prove you were wronged, you cannot have lasting positive relationships. You will show kindness only until you discover the other person's flaws, at which point the relationship will melt down.

Sharp discernment of someone else's sin is often a sign that you are personally very well practiced in that sin. It is quite common for people with pride to accuse others of pride, people with judgment to accuse others of judgment, and so forth. You think that by rebuking others, you are fixing yourself. What negative traits do you often notice in others? Are you the same way? (Rom. 2:21-22). This kind of discernment that sees all of the sins of others is not discernment at all. In reality, it is judgment and condemnation.

Many people are convinced their ability to see the sins of others is a "gift of discernment," but it is really a spirit of accusation. Does your gift ever tell you anything good about other people? When you use your "gift," are people set free of bondage, or do you find yourself isolated and in conflict? One of the most dramatic encounters our ministry had was when we cast the demon out of a man who was under this exact deception. We first had to show him that his entire life of "discernment" was really one of being a mouthpiece for Satan to accuse the brethren.

When judgments escalate, we become angry. Anger is a way of trying to force someone else to take the blame. In anger, you always magnify another person's sin while minimizing your own. It is your way of justifying yourself while accusing the other person. This makes you feel better at the expense of hurting someone else. How will they respond to you? They will try to force you to take the blame back by responding with anger of their own. This will escalate until one of you apologizes.

Some people with an anger problem hide behind the scripture to "be angry and do not sin" (Eph. 4:26) as if Paul was saying it's ok to be angry, or that as long as you do not actually act on it you are fine. They go on to claim they have "righteous anger." Righteous anger is based in love: love toward those who were hurt, love toward God and love toward the person you are angry at. I have never yet heard someone quote Ephesians 4:26 who was moving in this kind of spirit.

When we were running a recovery ministry, we never took in a single person who did not think everyone else in the house wa a bigger problem than they were. The reaction of one man I gave this book to is typical. After diving into the book, he called me excitedly to say, "This describes my wife exactly!" Even though this book talks from beginning to end about taking responsibility for yourself, he was only able to see her wrongs, not his own. If you have been reading this book with someone else in mind, stop here, go back to page one, and begin to examine yourself. That is the person who needs to change to improve your life.

Blame-shifting and pointing the finger is what allows people to avoid their problems long enough to hit bottom. Instead of taking the signals which come back as signs to change, they blame others or circumstances. We know when our participants begin to mature because they stop talking about what others need to change, and start talking about what they need to change. We know they are ready for life

> If you have been reading this book with someone else in mind, stop here and go back.

on their own when they are able to respond in a Christ-like fashion and diffuse conflicts instead becoming embroiled in them. Are you still more interested in other people's problems than your own? Are you still running through a mental list of how others are so hard to live with? When you hear a convicting sermon, do you apply it to yourself or do you sit there instead thinking, "Man, that *other* guy needs this message!"? It's time to look in the mirror. You are where you are because of the person you see staring back at you, and that is the person who needs to change to get you out of your trouble.

WHAT MOM AND DAD DID?

We mentioned how perhaps nothing is more fundamental to your freedom than learning to remove the log in your own eye. Remember Adam and Eve? They admitted to their "sin" but really blamed it on someone else. When you start obeying Jesus' command to deal with your own sin first, the anger and blaming stop. When you come to the point when you are not part of the problem at all, you will be operating in love and will not be looking for a person to blame.

Many people out there blame their parents for the way they are. Parents do have a major impact on their children, yet surprisingly few of the people who blame their parents for the ways in which they failed also thank them for the ways in which they succeeded. We live in a generation where it is popular to psychoanalyze your childhood to find the roots of all of your problems. In fact, some of those who had it best as children appreciate it least. No matter how bad your childhood was, somebody had to do something for you or you would not even be alive.

The root of your problems actually predates anything your parents did or didn't do. The ultimate root of all your problems is the sinful nature which you had when you were born. When you were born, you did not need to be taught to do evil; you did it naturally. You lied, hit, coveted, were selfish, and did all the corrupt things you see in children and teenagers around you today. You needed to be taught to do good. You were born with a desperate need to be trained to escape the deceitfulness of your own heart. This is something few people fully understand until they themselves are parents. Most parents use the best tools they know of to deal with sin and keep their kids from hurting themselves or others. Are you thankful for them, or are you blaming your problems on the ways they came up short?

Blaming your parents dishonors them and violates the 5th commandment. Unfortunately, even in the church this kind of dishonoring of parents is in vogue. When I was in high school I was fortunate enough to have a positive relationship with my parents. I couldn't really think of anything significant they had done wrong. I was thankful for them and everything they had done for me. In college, however, I attended an "inner healing" seminar designed to help me overcome personal bondages. Included in this seminar were large sections focusing on sins my parents might have handed down. By the time I left this seminar, I had learned to connect each of my shortcomings with a behavior or pattern learned at home. I saw my parents in a lesser light. In other words, I learned to dishonor my parents from church!

While I know those who were trying to help me meant well, archaeology about everything that happened in your past or mine is not really the solution. The issue is who I am now and how I can learn to be the person God made me to be. My parents spent eighteen years doing the best they could, and now I have access to the Fathering which comes from above. My earthly parents deserve a big "thank you" from me, not a list of grievances.

Of course many people are not nearly as fortunate as I was and grew up suffering real harm at the hands of their parents. If you are one of those people, you know it because you've carried around an obvious burden your whole life, not one you discovered through detailed investigation. For those clearly used or abused by parents, it is hard to let go. But forgiveness is the path to freedom and honoring them. Plenty of former abusees testify to this. If you do not forgive, you will chain yourself to their sins and doom yourself to sin against others. Forgiveness breaks the pattern.

Of course you can learn patterns of sin such as alcoholism or physical abuse from your parents, but instead of taking responsibility to forgive them and change yourself, the popular concept of "generational curses" has become a way for parents, or even ancestors, to take the blame for your sin. Based on Old Testament Scriptures which say God will visit the sins upon the children to the third and fourth generations, an entire theology has been built which puts the focus of repentance on your ancestors. This requires you to know some serious family history in order to really repent. What if you were adopted and don't know your birth parents? Should you just repent of random sins just in case?

Ezekiel 18 addresses this directly. Take a look at verse 20: "The son shall not suffer for the iniquity of the father, nor the father suffer for the iniquity of the son. The righteousness of the righteous shall be upon himself, and the wickedness of the wicked shall be upon himself." Even though familial patterns are sometimes carried forward from one generation to the next, the guilt and need for repentance are on the individual. Furthermore, even if generational curses do exist, when you were born again you were adopted as a son or daughter of the Most High, as a child of Abraham by faith. You are a new creation. The old has gone and new has come! (2 Cor. 5:17). You have a new lineage which is pure and spotless.

TRAPPED BY CIRCUMSTANCES

Overcoming parental blame is so fundamental because the attitude is woven into the very fabric of how you think. Closely related is your attitude toward other authorities and the world as a whole. You may blame the government, the church, or other social groups. All these forms of blame function in just the same way – they create an overarching excuse for why you cannot change. The sad thing about excuses like this is they make you feel better at the moment but worse in the long run. Is the government, church, or society going to change? No. You can only change you. As long as you have a reason why you can't change, you won't change. It's a recipe for permanent oppression.

The longer you try to avoid responsibility the higher the mountain of consequences stacks up. Because you're avoiding the root cause, they snowball and your situation gets worse. You are then in the miserable situation where the fruit of the original problem has become a new problem. You couldn't manage your addiction so you got deep into debt, but then when you wanted out of your addiction you were too depressed by the debt to see any hope to escape the addiction. Or you had a rebellion problem and lashed out in anger at all of your friends and family, but when you were ready to get right, no one was left to help or support you. In situations like these it's easy for things to seem hopeless. It's easy to say, "because of all of these problems I can't get free." What is harder to see is that when you make the heart transformation, many of these circumstances will start to reverse. Don't look at your circumstances and say, "I can't change because of these things." You still have a choice. If you and the devil can get into a mess, then you and God can get out of it.

What about circumstances that are completely beyond control? Some circumstances which are beyond control become reasons why we think we can't get free. We think, "If only I had never been in that accident, everything would be fine." Or, "If I hadn't been born in such-a-such place, with such-and-such parents, with such-and-such a condition, I'd have avoided all that pain." When I was 16, I was in a horrible accident which killed one of my friends and seriously injured two others including myself. What has always struck me about that tragedy, as I watched people involved grapple with it, is that the way each responded to the event made all the difference in the world. For some it became a source of permanent pain, but for others it was a source of power. For some it became a source of paralysis, but for others it was a source of action. How do you respond when circumstances turn against you?

> What really matters I not how far you have to climb, but whether you make the choice to climb at all.

What we learn from great hero stories and people like the Special Olympians is that what really matters is not how far you have to climb to overcome your circumstances, but whether you make the choice to climb at all. People with much smaller obstacles allow their whole lives to be frozen by something God can heal. Remember Romans 8:28? Its real teaching is you cannot blame circumstances for your problems because God is able to turn around every circumstance for His glory if you respond properly. Instead of a reason to pawn the problem off on God, it's a spur to take redemption action.

Even small excuses work against your freedom. Do you blame your bad attitude on a headache or cold, or on a long day at work? These things no doubt present challenges, but if you use them as excuses, the freedom you are seeking will elude you. You have to face it head-on to beat it. Realizing, "I am messed up," is not condemning – it is the powerful place of change which you must find to get free. When you reach that point, you realize you need a Savior. You are utterly dependent on Him to change. The good thing is He died to take your sin away. He doesn't just forgive you of it, but His love will actually take it out of your life, with all of its consequences.

IT WAS THE FLESH!

Some theologies actually seem to teach that when you sin, it isn't really you, it is your flesh, the "sinful nature," the "old man", or the "soul realm." The problem is when this becomes a new and more spiritual way of avoiding responsibility. You start to think the sin comes from somewhere else, by a different part of yourself that is supposedly dead. The problem is that if it is dead, then how did it sin? And if it sinned, what do you do about it? You are told nothing you can do affects your standing with God, because it was done by this other part of you that doesn't really count. Because it wasn't really you, you do not have to worry.

Well-meaning ministries have tried to build on this by telling you that if you want to be free, you just simply confess that you are free. This is skipping an important step, however: acknowledging that you sinned, and turning away from that sin and toward God.

Some will take it as far as saying that you should "renounce" sin instead of "repent." This implies you do not accept the reality of your sin, or your own responsibility for it. You cannot simply "renounce" sin as if it were a bad monkey on your back, or confess it away as if you didn't do it. The Biblical solution to removing sin is always repentance – a change of heart.

Our experience with this approach is that while it seems to offer an explanation for the problem, you will be disappointed with the result. You will expend a lot of energy trying to convince your mind of your freedom but never really cut away the power of sin. Sin does not happen in some other part of you that has no impact on your relationship to God or others. When you sin, you must take responsibility. If you want to be free from its power, you must repent of it.

Rebuking the sin or the flesh will not get you free. I am a strong believer that confessing the Word of God over your life as part of experiencing freedom, but a true confession is based in repentance. You put off the earthly, and then you put on the heavenly. Confessing the Word is supposed to be a way of turning away from sin, not a way of covering it up. It will not work until you have addressed the sin underneath.

THE DEVIL MADE ME DO IT

If it wasn't God or the flesh, it must have been the devil! Perhaps the greatest irony of the blame game is that blaming Satan for your problem ensures he will have power over you. That's right, the more you blame the devil, the more power he has. After Adam blamed Eve, what was her response? Did she own up to the problem and repent? No, she did exactly the same thing Adam had done – she blamed someone else. Only in this case, the someone else was Satan: "The serpent deceived me and I ate."

Demonic deliverance has become much more popular in the past 40 years than perhaps at any time in history, and it is undoubtedly a needed ministry. We started our ministry with an emphasis on removing the devil's influence from each person's life, and we still believe in it. However, after working with a number of people, a pattern emerged – the more unhealthy a person was, the more eager they were to have their problems "cast out." Instead of saying "I was feeling prideful," the person would say "A spirit of pride came on me." Instead of lusting after a woman, it was a "spirit of lust" that jumped on them. They were to have us try to "cast out" their demon because this does not require them to accept any responsibility for what is going on and make real changes. That is going nowhere. The "spirit of pride" will leave when the pride itself is gone from your heart.

At one point in my life, I was so distraught with my own lust problem that I drove to another city so I could go to a church where they specialized in deliverance. I went down to the altar and they rebuked the enemy, as I had done many times myself, but I went away just the same as before. The real change came only when my inner heart identity and love for sin changed. People who are heavily oppressed know the devil is real and oppressing them, so they seek ministry designed to attack the demonic. But the walk to lasting freedom is not primarily about Satan, it's about you and God. At the end of the day, what has to happen is a change in your heart.

Moreover, can you really cast out a "spirit of pride"? Our experience is that you cannot. You can yell and shout at the devil, you can speak in tongues and cry, but working with a house of guys focused on recovery allows us to see the long term effects of such encounters. Many deliverance ministries do not have the luxury of seeing the end-to-end perspective, and those which do realize most cases required repeated ministry because of the character issues which are always closely associated with demonic oppression. People seem encouraged for awhile, and then they go right back where they were. This is because you can't cast out your character!

Have we seen demons leave? Yes. But it happens when a person is ready to take responsibility and no longer wants any-thing to do with the sin the demon is associated with. People sometimes say to treat your sin as if it were a demon. This is backwards. You should treat your demon as if it is a sin. You are not a victim who has to accept its presence. You are a child of God with the power and responsibility to drive it out of your life. Deliverance can help, but it can only take you so far. It can get you a good breakthrough or deal with a wound from the past, but only when you apply the gospel to remove sinful beliefs from your heart will you obtain lasting freedom. The scriptural term for this is repentance.

Satan is glad to play the scapegoat because blaming him ensures you will not get free. In fact, blame empowers him. The most demonized people are the most consistently "victimized" by the devil. If you want out of Satan's grip, take control of yourself and get your focus on God. God made you the head and not the tail, and He gave you victory over Satan through the Cross. Remember, freedom begins when you deal with the real root of the problem – your sinful heart and behavior. Until you do this, rebuking the devil is chasing after the wind.

One of the ways Satan creates bondage is by acting omnipresent in your life. He does things to draw attention to himself, make himself seem big and scary, and generally mouth off all the time to get you to focus on him. The more focus he gets, the more power he gets. So while asserting your authority over Satan is definitely a part of the freedom process, it is most certainly not the focus. The focus is on you getting right with God. For those with heavy oppression, this is one of the hardest parts. Their life experience is full of voices and feelings that come from Satan, so their vocabulary and way of thinking is all about "attacks" and "what the devil did." While this is perfectly understandable, it is not helpful.

> The fact that you are alive shows how little power Satan really has over your life.

My experience is that those with voices experience the same temptations, feelings, and thoughts that those without voices do — they just hear and listen to what the devil is saying better. They attribute power in their lives to Satan. They fear what Satan might do to them. They think Satan gives some things to them and takes others away. It's like the man who bought himself some new audio equipment but thought the devil "let him" do it. Satan does not "let" you do anything. It is all a web of deception designed to make Satan the god of your world. If he could kill you he would. Since you are alive, that shows how little power he really has in your life. Getting out of the cycle of bondage means breaking out of thought patterns which turn attention to Satan and getting into ones that turn attention toward God. It's about closing down your heart to sin and temptation, and putting your mind on the things of God.

Don't give the devil a part in the movie that isn't his. It's not about you and Satan, it's about you and God.

In fact, I have found some of the teachings associated with the idea of spiritual warfare unintentionally empower the devil. When we look at things that happen to us as an "attack" we are ascribing power to Satan to do us harm. The Bible says Jesus made an "open showing" of the devil and "all authority" on heaven and earth was given to Jesus. Ascribing power to Satan gives him power because through fear, we exalt his ability to harm us. You become focused on how he operates and how his kingdom works, and then he, instead of Christ, becomes the center of your religion. You spend your days rebuking and casting out, but nowhere in the Bible do we see this lifestyle modeled. Jesus and the apostles lived a life of authority and surpassing personal peace. We see them rebuke demons off of heavily demonized people, but the substance and focus of their religious experience was God. Jesus feared absolutely nothing – the demons tremble at his name, not the other way around.

This has even been taken as far as rebuking principalities and power of the air – in other words, rebuking high ranking demonic powers who have influence over regions. First, it is unclear from the Bible if these powers exist in the way we have been taught they do. Secondly, assuming they do, it is Jesus' promise that He will bind them in heaven if we bind them on earth. This means if we disciple the minds of God's people, reach lost souls, and salt the culture of the world, such principalities will have no authority to operate. We rob Satan's kingdom of subjects and principalities of their power. As the Kingdom of God spreads over the whole earth, Satan's kingdom is diminished.

So the name of the game, whether personal or corporate, is not really about rebuking Satan, it is about taking away his power through repentance and the exaltation of God. As you exalt God and ascribe power to Him, you give Him more power in your life. That's why worship songs are about Jesus. As you lift Him up, He reforms your heart and becomes God of your life. He is the one with power, not Satan.

So what does the devil actually do? He presents you with opportunities to sin. He stirs up your emotions toward sin to supercharge these choices if we're open to it. He plays the endless tape of evil thoughts in your mind if you let him. He will intimidate you through fear, and push you into compulsive thoughts and feelings. He does these things to make it harder to escape. But remember, ultimately the power to escape is in your faith in God and you taking responsibility for your own action. As the father of lies, Satan invents all kinds of falsehoods to keep you from seeing the truth of God. He cannot make you sin, and he cannot pull you away from God. You just have to make the choice who to believe.

Most importantly Satan does everything he can to convince you God is the problem. This is why for those under deep bondage, the number one item on his list is to try to make them say something horrible to God and convince them they have blasphemed the Holy Spirit. He wants enmity between you and God because he knows God is your only way out. And for most people in heavy oppression, this is exactly what they are struggling with most. They struggle to believe God really does love them, that they really are forgiven. Satan wants you in a relationship with him instead of God. He wants you fearing him, rebuking him, and otherwise keeping him on your mind because by being in relationship with him he can keep you in bondage. On the other hand when you begin to believe God is the answer and you begin to put all of your focus on His love, you seat yourself far above any place where Satan can touch you.

The End of Mysticism

One of the reasons many people cannot connect their symptoms to the root cause is because they have embraced systems of belief which are not logical. These belief systems short-circuit the sin-discovery process by attacking the role of human cause and effect. In the place of cause and effect you have a "mystery" -- a system which allows confusion to exist in your heart and doctrine. This confusion keeps you chasing after the wind, as the truth is just beyond your grasp.

Thankfully, not everything you think is a mystery is really a mystery. In the New Testament, Paul actually looks upon the church age as the time for mysteries to be revealed, not concealed (Eph 1:9; Col 1:25-26). The things we really need to know – how to be saved and how to live free, are made plain in the New Testament.

MYSTERIES OF SATAN'S KINGDOM

Even though we live in the age when mysteries have been revealed, many Christians are still addicted to seeking myterious special knowledge. Some Christians have become convinced that knowing more about Satan's Kingdom is the way to defeat Satan. The Bible, after all, provides very little direct knowledge of how Satan and the occult operate. Perhaps the Biblical question to ask here is: Can Satan drive out Satan? (Mat 12:26). You may think you are learning more about Satan's Kingdom in order to have power over him, but in fact just the opposite happens. The more you focus on the devil, the less you focus on God, and the more power Satan can have over you.

In the last 30 years people have circulated the church claiming revelation about everything occult—from what it is like to be a vampire, to how to escape from being a Satanic High Priestess.

Not only have many of these people been proven to be charlatans, but the whole enterprise is faulty because such knowledge is more occult in nature than Christian. If God needed us to know how Satan's kingdom operated in detail, he would have provided more detail in Scripture. Many of us need the same rebuke Jesus gave the church of Thyatira—for having "learned what some call the deep things of Satan" (Rev. 2:24). God wants you to be fascinated with Him and in knowing Him more. Satan is defeated by you knowing God more, not by you knowing more about Satan!

> Satan is defeated by you knowing God more, not by you knowing more about Satan.

Some deliverance ministries have unwittingly contributed to this occult focused thinking. By placing emphasis on sins of the past or ancestry, people become convinced there is an inherited demonic reason why they cannot have freedom. They believe they must close an unknown door or renounce an unknown sin in order to experience freedom. Ironically, instead of freeing people from the occult, this can often lead people deeper into special occult knowledge. Because you need special information in order to get free, you end up learning about the occult to get that special information. People in this trap learn about Satanic ritual abuse, special rites of the Freemasons, the Kundalini effect, transcendental meditation, and every other kind of bizarre ritual in hopes that breaking one of these will provide their victory. In the best case this is a distraction, or in the worst case, some kind of "Christian" spell-casting: pray this special prayer and you will suddenly be a different person.

In truth, knowledge about the dark world does not hold the key to your freedom. Satan wants you to think he is powerful and that breaking his curses off your life is a difficult, intricate process requiring all kinds of special insight. It is all a demonic illusion. When you believe he has power over you, he will have it. Jesus broke the power of the devil. It's not your ancestor's demonic past that is holding you in bondage; it is what is going on in your heart now. Can an occult past have an influence on your life? Yes, if it is part of your life now. Ironically, for people with an occult past, this kind of Christian knowledge of the dark kingdom is simply continuing in the same occult mentality which put them in bondage in the first place. Their focus on the forces of darkness is what gives the forces of darkness power in their lives! I'm not saying the devil's voices and attacks aren't real, but your fear of them is what gives them power. Christ is seated far above every ruler, authority, and spell that can be cast on you. You need to learn how to abide in Him, not how to do a Christian magic trick.

MYSTERIES BEYOND YOUR CONTROL

Any theory of the world which moves agency away from you or humanity is another kind of mystery. This can come in the form of a conspiracy theory or even Biblical doctrine where instead of placing responsibility on individuals to act, responsibility is ascribed to some hidden actor or group. The focus moves away from you and onto some theory about where the real power lies. It dismantles and confuses cause and effect. But the connection between cause and effect is what you need to have a victorious Christian walk. Once you connect your agency with change, you suddenly begin to change things.

For example, some Christians love to learn about supposed conspiracies running the world. There are a myriad of theories ranging from Illuminati to Freemasons, from socialist to capitalist cabals. Not only are such theories unprovable by nature, they undermine God's role as the master strategist of history. The Bible says "all authority" has been given to Jesus (Matt. 28:18) and His government will always increase (Is. 9:7). Regardless of minor conspiracies then, the real march of history is Jesus' progressive victory over Satan's kingdom. To those lost in conspiracy theory God says, "Do not call conspiracy all that this people calls conspiracy" (Is. 8:1). Unprovable knowledge available only to a select few is not Christianity—it's paganism.

Another kind of mysticism has crept into the church from New Age philosophy posing as science. A theory based on a misunderstanding of quantum physics suggests your mind determines physical reality. You are thought to have power through your mind rather than through your actions. This leads you down a path of mental gymnastics as you try to cause things to happen by thinking them. It also leads to an inflated sense of self, as if you were able to control things you cannot. At the same time it confuses cause and effect, it takes your focus away from what will really change your life – action that is based on faith.

You can see a similar phenomenon in the church where some have become very interested in the supposed details of how the End Times are unfolding. You learn as much as you can about what the Bible and various interpreters say so that you can be ready when Jesus returns. The problem is that, more often than not, this is a distraction. Instead of doing God's work in your life, you are caught up in a system of interpretation where God, Satan, and the antichrist do all the work. Jesus' clear teaching on this subject is, "The Son of Man is coming at an hour you do not expect... Blessed is that servant whom his master will find so doing when he comes." (Matthew 24:44,46). What we know is that Jesus is coming and we'd better be about the Master's business, not sitting around guessing when it's going to happen. Jesus will return when we have reached every tribe, every tongue, and every nation with His liberating gospel (Matt. 24:14, Rev. 5:9). We've been on the job for 2000 years and huge progress has been made, but the mission is not complete.

These are just a few of a seemingly endless number of ways you can become sidetracked by seeking special knowledge instead of growing in the knowledge of God. In fact, this problem is as old as the gospel itself. Paul confronts it directly in 1 Timothy 6:20 when he says, "Avoid the irreverent babble and contradictions of what is falsely called 'knowledge.'" Having more information or teachings makes us feel smarter and appeals to your pride but it does not lead to freedom. It leads to distraction and bondage.

THE MYSTERIOUS GOD

Mysticism can also creep into your ideas about God and how you relate to Him. Some are enamored with conceptions of God from Eastern Orthodoxy, Catholic mystics, apocryphal gospels, or Jewish Kabbalah. These all celebrate God as unknowable, remote, or incomprehensible. By not understanding, you are said to be getting in touch with the divine. Certainly God's infinity is far beyond our grasp, but at the same time, Jesus died on the Cross so we could have a real, knowable, and living relationship with God—not a distant, mysterious one. Mystery focuses on the unknowable, but Christianity focuses on a Christ who is knowable.

Other Christian circles use "mystery" as a way of covering for a misconception of God. They tell us God chooses some to be saved and some to be damned, but when we ask how a loving God can do this, we are told it is a "mystery." We are told that "God's ways are higher than our ways." In other words, it is so illogical to say a loving God chooses people for hell that no-one can provide any rational explanation for it and it must be a mystery. Is God's love really so completely different from human love as to be incomprehensible?

In addition, because these same Christians view God as being in control of absolutely everything, the same question arises as to why evil occurs. The logical answer in this system would be to blame God, but since you can't do that, they say it is a "mystery" why bad things happen. This is a problem created by a false idea of God. The obvious answer is that bad things happen because of sin, not because of God. Mystery in this case is just another word for a doctrine that is illogical and misrepresents God. God reveals himself in the Bible as perfectly loving and perfectly knowable. When you encounter a "mystery" that makes God distant, you've encountered a lie.

On the other end of the spectrum, some people have developed what I call the Christian "lotto" mentality. Things seem so bleak that they feel their only hope is to win the God lottery. God will come down and suddenly strike, and they will be free! Does God do this? Yes, absolutely. However, you cannot make a poor man rich by winning the lottery. Many people who win the lottery experience significant misery after winning, and are quickly poor all over again. This is because they did not know how to manage a little money when they were poor. How much less can they manage a huge sum of money when they are rich?

Managing your spiritual life is quite similar. Sadly, people in bondage who experience a dramatic and sudden God breakthrough often do not build on it to walk all the way to freedom. Usually they wait until that breakthrough runs out, and then wait for another breakthrough to get them out again. If God were to suddenly give them the same breakthrough, they would keep up this pattern. You cannot be free living this way. Whether it is a delivering or ministering experience in the past you wish you could have again, or an experience you think would make it all go away, the problem is you end up waiting on God to do something dramatic instead of taking progressive steps to freedom. All the time and energy you spent chasing the experience could have instead been used to move you down the road toward long-term freedom.

> You are waiting on God to do something dramatic instead of taking progressive steps to freedom.

I am totally for God breakthroughs, but whether you have one or not, your ultimate victory is going to come by progressive steps over the long haul. As you steward your own spiritual life, you will learn the skills you need to maintain permanent freedom. The solution is not somewhere out there; it is right where you are sitting.

The flavor of some contemporary preaching can lead you to believe that aside from any action on your part except faith and possibly making a check out to the preacher, something will happen to change your situation. Powerful preaching releases faith, but real faith begins with repenting and taking action. When you remove these, faith becomes mystical. Don't get me wrong, faith is crucial and great preaching can build it like nothing else, but when preaching intentionally or unintentionally disconnects your faith from your action, you've got mysticism. Faith without works is dead (Jas. 2:17). It isn't real.

What if I was broke because I went to the casino but I was "believing God" for a new house and "sowed in" my last dollar to the offering. Even though my unrepentant gambling is completely wrong, I have a mystical belief which tells me my faith will come through anyway. Then when someone in church feels sorry for me and buys me dinner, I think my miracle has come through! Actually it was a human being showing me mercy.

The worst part about this kind of "faith" worldview is it's a substitute for being changed. It's a placebo that makes you feel like you are being changed. Because you are feeling confident and seeing the world through a lens of positive expectation, you avoid the areas in your life which are really holding you in bondage. I'm not saying you shouldn't believe God for the impossible. What I am saying is if the gambler were really in faith, he would repent of gambling, develop some saving habits, and then believe God for the miracle financial breakthrough. There is no doubt God is able to do over and above anything you can dream, but He is not operating a cosmic slot machine – He works in conjunction with the reformation of your character.

LEADINGS

Some people interpret the Biblical command to be led by the Spirit to mean God has to control their every move. This too will lead you into mysticism. You will look for a special "word" or "leading" to tell you what to do. You will look for a special "anointing" to enable you to do powerful, spiritual acts. You will look for a special deliverance church, minister, or experience to set you free from the sin in your life. These tools are all valid but none of them are the focus of the Christian life. The attitude that drives a "leading" mentality is one where you are relying on a special act of God in order for you to move forward. But special acts are exactly that: special.

When you are looking for that special touch, it's natural to try and chase God by going from one prophetic conference to another. I was like this myself for several years after I had a life changing encounter with God at a prophetic conference. I kept trying to find and experience the same thing I did at the first meeting. The only problem was that such meetings could never take me from where I was to the place I wanted to be. I would hear extensive details about angelic encounters and visits to heaven, and I began to believe the focus of the Christian life was in having these encounters. Some take it even farther, and have become enamored with gold dust, gemstones and other manifestations. Eventually I realized this pursuit was not taking me any closer to the intimate and heavenly lifestyle I desired. I was pursuing signs of God, but He was pursuing my heart. Perhaps Paul had someone like me in mind when he said, "Let no one keep defrauding you of your prize by delighting in ...the worship of the angels, taking his stand on visions he has seen, inflated without cause by his fleshly mind" (Col. 2:18). We have to be careful not to confuse the pursuit of spiritual phenomena with the pursuit of God.

In this prophecy-oriented phase of my life I would go from one prophetic church to another seeking a cooler word. Having a prophetic word in your life can be very powerful, but needing to live from one prophecy to the next shows a fundamental misunderstanding of the purpose of revelation. Revelation does not dictate the future or divine a course of action – it *reveals* the character of your heart. It is relational in nature – God reveals something and offers you a choice. Revelation exhorts you to make a choice to move in the right direction.

What is far more important than the revelation itself is the context into which it is spoken. The prophetic word to a man living in adultery is going to be fundamentally different from the word given to a man totally surrendered to God. Revelation is spoken into the context of your life, and that context is determined not by the prophetic words spoken over you, but by the actions you have taken based on your heart. In other words, what is in your heart is the real driver of your life.

God uses revelation to speak to and redirect your heart, not as a substitute for your own volition. This is because simply following revelation around allows you to remain unchanged and perform only outward obedience. Even the demons had this kind of outward obedience to Christ in response to His word. Being united with Christ means you are called to obey from the heart. That's what Jesus wants from us: obedience which stems not from giving more and more directions, but obedience that stems from being of one heart and mind with Him. By moving from one prophecy to the next, you avoid the real work of becoming like and following Christ on a heart level.

I am reminded of a woman my wife once counseled. She was totally enamored with an older, divorced man whom she discovered was playing the field with a variety of other women. After receiving extensive counsel on why she needed to stop pursuing this man because he would ruin her life, she still wanted to know if we had received a prophetic word telling her what to do! Either she was living by leadings and ignoring reality, or she was only open to a prophecy that would tell her what she wanted to hear. This is a dangerous attitude. There will always be a false prophet, or false friend available to prophesy to the idol of your heart and tell you what your itching ears want to hear. Do you allow people around you who will tell you the truth you don't like?

In reality, we all make wrong choices in life because we are blinded by sin. Someone comes along that you just "don't feel right about" and yet you do business with them anyway. After they steal your money, you wonder how you could have been so foolish. You were foolish because you refused to believe what you conscience was telling you. Maybe you refused because you were greedy and wanted the money. Maybe you refused because you believed the partner was a "good person." Maybe you refused because you didn't listen to a trustworthy voice in you life. Ultimately, you refused to hear the warning because you did not ask God or listen to the clear witness of the Spirit working through your conscience.

Special revelation works in concert with what you know to be true through your understanding of God's principles and the witness of his Spirit in your heart. Do you have a word that you are holding on to, in spite of your own best judgment and the counsel of friends? For years, I felt trapped in a church because I felt that I had been prophesied in and could not leave unless I had another subsequent prophecy. There were warning signs all around me that I needed to leave, but I ignored them partly because I was waiting on another word for new direction. Finally I got one and it said, "What are you waiting for?" The joke was on me. I had been so afraid to take action without a word that I had ignored the everyday signs telling me for years I needed to move on.

Some people are not chasing a word; they are chasing a "destiny." Maybe you were told when you got saved that God would fulfill your "destiny." In these destiny stories you may imagine yourself in super-significant places like Esther, Daniel, or Joseph, with the fate of civilization hanging on you. You may imagine you will rise to the top of your field or do something ultra-crucial in God's Kingdom: you will lead millions to Christ, and preach in stadium crusades all around the world. You may have even received extravagant prophecies confirming your ministry "to the nations." This kind of thinking appeals to pride, posturing you as more important than others. It replaces what you do for Christ for who you are in Christ. The impossibly great destiny scenarios are just not real for the vast majority of people. Most of us are plumbers, bankers, and office workers, not popes and presidents.

The destiny concept also presupposes that such prominent roles are more important to God. Yet Jesus clearly teaches that what matters is not how prominent you are, but that you are totally surrendered to God (Mark 1:35-45). In the Bible, Isaac was just a guy with two kids who lived in the desert. Was he less significant than Joseph or Esther? Freedom is found not in holding up the idol of a destiny but in a lifestyle which is totally devoted to God, whatever your situation is. Pursuing God with your whole heart and making the greatest use of the talents and experiences He has given you are the best ways to find your "destiny."

A related pursuit for the perfect and unattainable is finding your "soul mate." Maybe it's too many Cinderella stories, but some people who are otherwise completely rational decision makers lose all sense of logic when they start thinking about a potential future spouse. They ignore warning signs, get confirmation dreams, put out fleeces, and continually ask themselves, "Is this person *the one*?" Sometimes church culture reinforces this. I used to go to a church where finding your spouse was supposed to come with signs and wonders. Prophetic marriages were the rule of the day, but some of the ones with the most prophecies were some of the craziest – including the pastor who left his first prophetic marriage before finding the second one. Some people even think their real "soul mate" is already married to someone else. There are no limits on how inappropriate these scenarios can become.

The simple fact is that marriage is a decision of one man and one woman to spend the rest of their lives together. Proactively seeking a godly person of the opposite sex who will follow God with you, wherever he leads, and raise a strong family with you is the best way to find your "soul mate." Looking for "*the* one" is a chase after the wind. If you are looking to be married, the better question is, "Is someone around me who I can build a godly life with? If not, how can I find one?" This may seem less exciting or less spiritual, but it will lead to a happy ending.

If life were a chess match, it would be your move. Pursuit of special directions, destinies, soul mates, and the like reflect a misunderstanding of revelation. Although God knows the end from the beginning, remember that is not what revelation is really about. It's about God helping you walk through life toward him. Your heart is what drives your decision making and takes you places in life. As you turn away from sin and submit to God in deeper and more significant ways, the direction of your life will change. As the direction of your life changes, the context into which a prophetic word comes will change. The focus of the gospel is making you like Jesus on a heart level, and following directions alone cannot do that. I do not chase words, anointings, or deliverance anymore. I know if I allow Christ in me to rule, I will have all of these things when I need them; and when I do not, God is still with me every step.

Lest I be misunderstood, let me be emphatic in saying that walking with the Holy Spirit is not only crucial to the Christian life, but one of life's greatest joys. I am not advocating a return to a Christianity which only informs the mind. I believe in and practice the miraculous gifts of 1 Corinthians 12. I am not advocating cutting out the prophetic out of your life. Prophecy can be a powerful aid to a successful Christian life. What I am saying is that walking with the Holy Spirit and even having a supernatural lifestyle work together with having your mind engaged.

Moreover, what all of these "mystery" theologies have in common is they short circuit the process of human reason and initiative. They are answers that do not add up. When the Holy

Spirit comes in power, He does so in response to faith and action. He does things that may not make sense to us looking forward, but do make sense to us looking backward. Many of us have been taught doctrines which lead us to believe the more irrational the behavior is, the more likely it is God. Or you believe inexplicable things which you cannot influence must happen in order to get you free. If such is the case, then why teach at all? You can't teach the irrational. Why seek at all? You can't pursue something inexplicable.

Christianity is about eliminating unknowable mysteries shrouded in illogical darkness and moving into His marvelous light. The discoverers of science knew this. Contrary to thousands of years of mysticism, they found principles by which the world operates. They found them

> Coming into freedom means leaving mysticism behind.

because they believed a knowable God had made a world that could be known. Instead of a demon-haunted wood run by strange, mysterious, spiritual phenomena, they found a rational world set up by an orderly, supernatural God. True revelation reveals. It brings clarity. It works in conjunction with reason, not against it. Coming into a place of freedom means leaving mysticism behind. This will expose hidden things in your life, bring clarity to the confusion that has you walking around in circles, and most importantly, put the ball back in your court.

Get Real

Although blame is the most obvious avoidance strategy, it is not the only one. Going back to the Garden of Eden, you will remember that before the blame game ever started, Adam and Eve realized something was wrong and made coverings for themselves from fig leaves (Gen. 3:7). In other words, covering your sin is the most natural thing in the world, but it is at the core of the problem.

THE IMAGE

Most people have built up an elaborate image of how they want other people to see them. In fact, I have come to learn that this is the normal psychology of the world. The inner thought life of someone who is healthy and free is based on being real, but for someone who is in bondage, it is based on making sure that other people have a positive impression of you. You go to great lengths to build up and feed this image so you can continue

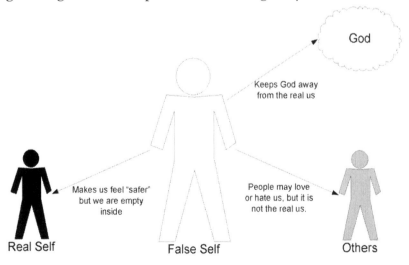

God

Keeps God away
from the real us

Makes us feel "safer"
but we are empty
inside

People may love
or hate us, but it is
not the real us.

Real Self

False Self

Others

to be accepted by others or feel worthy when you look in the mirror. The Biblical word for this image is an idol. This false self is an idol – an imaginary perfect person who stands between you, God, and others. Anything not meeting expectations or worthy of approval is not part of the idol. It remains in the dark shadow of who you really are, where you do not allow others, even God, to access. Whenever this idol begins to crack, you feel exposed and will work frantically to patch it up. You think the idol you have built keeps you safe and accepted, but in reality it keeps you far away from others.

We develop and prop up idols because of deep insecurities. This may have originated at home, if little affirmation was given to you, or if you were affirmed but did not hear or receive it. The Darwinistic treatment we receive in social settings is often what seals the deal, however. Growing up, you are mocked for being yourself so you learn to be someone else in order to be accepted by peers. Even though you grow out of these situations, you do not grow out of need to conform to the standards of others in order to get approval. This socialization is ultimately designed to make you submitted to the opinions of others rather than the opinion of God. People in the world condemn you when you show weakness, so you learn not to show it.

For some people, this idolatry runs very deep. You run from any church, situation, relationship or doctrine which will expose your real self, because it is too painful and scary. The sad irony, however, is that your idol, like all idols, is a cruel taskmaster. It takes a massive amount of work to maintain. If you have this kind of idol, you probably feel tired after being around other people because you have to spend so much effort looking good for them or pleasing them. After a while in this game, your real self becomes lost. Your own emotions and identity get lost in the big show you are putting on for everyone else.

The idol also leads you into relationship with other people who have the same idol. This can be quite dangerous. When you hold up the idol, you're saying you are only comfortable in relationships where you know what is expected of you. As long as the other person gives you a list of expectations, you know you can meet them and be approved. Are you real with other people, or are you always trying to figure out how you need to act in order to impress them?

The only people you can impress this way are ones you do not want to impress. People who really love you will be impressed when you get real. They will probably want to get real too, and you'll finally feel some real love flowing back and forth in the relationship.

You must tear down the false self you are using to try to please people if you want to have authentic relationships with God and others. God does not heal idols – He's in the business of smashing them. Reality can be scary and even strange at first. When you encounter a person who wants to be real and expects you to be real in return, it feels scary – there is no image to protect you. Following a list of expectations seems safe, but being in a transparent and open relationship seems scary. What if you can't measure up? How can you, unless you know what you're measuring up to?

The irony is that people who want you to be transparent are often the ones who really love you. Those who put image expectations on you often have their own agendas and may even abuse you. They do not care about the real you; they just want you to do what is expected. People who really care about you want to know the real you, want to minister when you're weak, and usually feel connected through vulnerability. It may be difficult to become vulnerable because someone has taken advantage of your vulnerability in the past, but the path toward healing is finding trustworthy people and getting real with them.

Maybe your idol is not about impressing people, it's about intimidating them. You are hard. You do not allow yourself to feel or display emotions because that would show weakness. You simply shut them down. You think as long as you are on the attack, you can't be hurt. But in reality, everything you dish out comes right back. Being hard will not protect you at all. It simply isolates you from others and God. When you lash out at people, they lash back. When you shut others out, they shut you out. When you become unfeeling, you attract only the company of other unfeeling people. When you become "hard," you signal to others that you do not need or want anything. Perhaps you think you do not, but in order to be human, you must allow God to change your heart of stone to a heart of flesh (Ez. 11:19).

ACCOUNTABILITY AND LIES

Some ministries, understanding the human propensity to cover up, have created heavy regimes of accountability and confession to ensure you are transparent and not covering up your sin. Ironically, these regimes tend to produce just the opposite result! The more you know others are going to rake you over the coals for your sin, the more committed you become to hiding it. Instead of having conviction leading to repentance, you become full of man-made guilt which leads to more sin! The higher you move in the accountability hierarchy, the more committed you become to keeping up the image to cover it, and often, the deeper the hidden sin becomes. Lacerating people for their failings and putting strict accountability codes on them will not fix their problems because those are the acts of man, not the grace of God. Accountability only works if it helps you become more real with others, more real with yourself, and most importantly, more real with God. When you start to tear down the idol you have built for yourself, then others can love the real you, and God can heal the real you.

When the idol starts to crack, there is often a strong temptation to lie in order to keep it propped up. This is a slippery and dangerous road. Your word and testimony about yourself are the most valuable things you have. Once you lose them, you lose the trust of others. The lies may help you look good for a little bit, but soon enough people will find out the truth. In fact, if you are a habitual liar, chances are everyone already knows and just hasn't said so to your face. They no longer believe the things you say. As the lies go deeper, you begin to believe them yourself. You become foggy on what actually happened because the "truth" for you is whatever you think will make you look good in the moment. This stage of lying is like losing your soul. You don't know who

> You have to decide that what people think of you does not matter anymore.

you are and neither does anyone else. You are lost in the web of your own deceit.

You may fool some people, but Jesus is the Truth, and He is not fooled by all the lies. Lying ends when you decide you would rather look like a complete fool and be right with God. You are telling lies because you are trying to avoid looking bad or having to take responsibility. By doing this you are avoiding the very thing that will bring you real freedom! If you are in deep, you may need to get radical. Start telling everyone around you all of the lies you have told them and tear down that idol while you have the motivation. Some will reject you and be angry, but most people will actually be relieved and like you more when you start telling the truth. You have to decide that what people think of you does not matter anymore. What matters more than anything is having your soul back.

THE END OF THE COVER UP

Adam and Eve made their own coverings because they were naked and ashamed. Their sin had made them unable to be naked before God. What they had to do in order to be free was to allow God to remove their manmade coverings and replace them with his God-made garment (Gen 3:21) Nothing has changed since then. If you want to be free and have an intimate relationship with God and His people, you will need to do the same thing – get real. A relationship with God and with Christians demands that you show weakness and vulnerability. You do not have to be terrified that God or others will see who you really are because Jesus has dealt with the condemnation of sin through the Cross.

Failure to deal with the cover up is what is fundamentally backwards about many of popular ideas about Christianity. There are many methods of dealing with sin that do not actually deal with it. There are many methods of relating to God that do not require relationship! It's safer to keep God at a distance, since a real relationship with God will require you to change in very fundamental ways. The simple fact of encountering God is transforming, and many people simply do not want to change in the most important ways. When you do not want to change, you must keep God at a distance, and that is what many of our religious practices are designed to do. You can pray a prayer, say a positive confession, and be respected at church, all without having to change at a heart level.

Before you can be healed, you have to be prepared to get real. To the extent you're ready to do this reflects your true willingness to pursue freedom. Having worked with a number of people with this problem, I have learned this is a transition you cannot make overnight. It's more like an addiction. You are addicted to the security provided by the idol, and the approval it wins for you. And this can be a very strong drug, one which can drive you to do almost anything. By contrast, people who are transparent may seem strange, scary, uncool, or uninteresting. Because of this, I have found that people who start down the path of transparency often give up after a couple of weeks. The pain and insecurity they have been covering up inside for so long has become so great that facing it seems impossible. If this is you, then what you need is a *long term* commitment to being real, and developing real relationships. You need a commitment to facing and allowing God to heal the pain and insecurity. Old friends will probably reject you, but the new ones you get will love you for who you are.

Pride

Pride is another angle that you can look at what Adam and Eve did in the garden. When they sinned, they covered up, and then instead of relying upon God to resolve the problem, they took it upon themselves to resolve it. Their coverings were man-made. This is the essence of what pride is. It is any man-made form of significance. This significance becomes a substitute for God's significance.

Are you proud or are you humble? Pride celebrates who you are, but humility rests in the perfect love of God for you. Humility is recognizing you are a sinner, you are loved by God, and you are equal in value to everyone else. Pride is concerned about how you appear, but humility cares about how you love. Humility is being transparent, vulnerable, and authentic. Humility is knowing that you do not need to impress anyone. Becoming humble and getting real are therefore really part of the same process. It means casting down the false image you have created to protect yourself from the insecurity you feel, and the criticism of others.

If you value yourself by what you do or how you look, then this will become your god. You can see this in the lives of those who are slaves trying to climb corporate or government ladders. You can also see it in the church, in pastors who need to run larger and more impressive churches in order to feel significant. On the other hand, you can also see it in the lives of those who are depressed over their lack of success. They do not have corporate success or large ministries, but wish they did.

Some people, realizing they cannot pull value from what they do, how much money they have, or what others think of them, derive their value by proxy. You are attracted to the most radical or "cutting edge" people because it gives you a sense of significance. Because those people seem to have their act together and are doing the "next big thing," you are eager and jump on board. This is your pride. Do you feel your movement or corner of God's Kingdom is better than someone else's? This kind of ecclesial elitism is at the core of every known cult and many false doctrines. Certain people think by having special knowledge or association with the "real thing," that they are better, more significant, or more secure. In reality, they have moved away from the real root of the gospel, which is security and significance in Jesus Himself.

God points out in Psalm 115:4-7 that idols are deaf and blind. If you have an idol, it means you are unable to hear or see the truth. This is why Jesus says repeatedly in the gospels, "He who has ears to hear let him hear" (cf. Matt. 11:15, 13:9). Hearing is not the physical ability to hear or the mental ability to understand. Hearing is the process of listening to what someone else says, taking it in, and being transformed by it. If you are prideful then instead of hearing and being transformed, you have already made up your mind and will not allow wisdom from others to sway you. A prideful person is in dialogue not with the mind of God or the thoughts of others, but with him or herself. It is like the Pharisee whom Jesus describes as praying "to himself" (Luke 18:11).

Take a look at yourself: how do you respond when someone speaks the truth into your life? Do you get defensive? Do you feel belittled? Do you think the other person is being arrogant? Do you outwardly receive it but then when the pressure is on, reassert yourself? Do you catalog it away with all the other things you should believe but take no action? Do you simply ignore them? When someone speaks real truth into your life, you should be convicted. You should consider what they say and whether it is true. If it is true, even just a little, you should repent and change. If you do not, pride is stopping you.

The simplest litmus test for pride is this: When godly people tell you things, do you hear them? Do you change, or do you continue to do it your own way, thinking you've got it all figured out? A humble person takes correction to heart the first time, but the prideful person hears it over and over again while never changing. Does someone who is correcting in love make you feel humiliated? That quick feeling is also a sign of pride. The humble person hears the truth and is able to change because they would rather have the truth than anything else.

In fact, there is nothing more fundamental to freedom than developing the ability to hear. The people around you aren't even going to bother telling you the truth about yourself until you are willing to hear it. If someone knows you will get all offended when they tell you the truth, then most people will simply not tell you. They will avoid you instead. This means that by being unwilling to hear the truth, you create a vacuum around yourself. Your idol "protects" you from the truth. I don't care what your doctrine is, it's worthless until you are ready to hear and be changed by the truth.

The proud person is deaf because they think they have it figured out better than others. They are always thinking negative thoughts about others, and usually judge themselves as better. When someone like this sees their pride for the first time, it is often staggering. A great sermon on pride is much more likely to convict a few humble people of their need to be more humble than the proud. You may be reading this section thinking it is written for someone else, but that is often a good sign it's for you. Pride is completely blinding this way.

The prideful person is "always learning but never able to come to the knowledge of the truth" (2 Tim. 3:7). You learn more and more information, but it is simply head knowledge. You never repent and apply it to yourself. This is because "knowledge puffs up but love edifies" (1 Cor. 8:1). You may even be able to give expert counsel to someone else while your own life is in shambles in the very same area! Would you take your car to a mechanic who could not fix his own car? Knowing the answer and actually applying the answer are two different things. You do need basic correct information about God and sin to get free, but this information will avail you nothing if you do not apply it to yourself. It is the experience of putting your faith in practice that gives you real wisdom and qualification to help others.

FALSE HUMILITY

Most people think pride is only for people who think highly of themselves, but if you have a low opinion of yourself, you are in pride too. Sometimes this is called false humility. It's false because you and others may think you are humble. But it is a deception. In fact, some of the most prideful people we have ever ministered to were those who barely had a penny to their name and thought of themselves as worthless. What links outward and inward pride is the inability to hear others, and the need to compare yourself. Anytime you engage in comparisons with others, it shows you are not getting your value from God, but from your own opinion.

You may have a case against yourself in your head. In reality, this is Satan's view of you which you have embraced. He is the one accusing you day and night, who hates you because you are the image of God on earth. Low self-worth is agreeing with Satan about who you are. As long as you are agreeing with Satan you cannot be free. God does not see you according to your past or even your present. God sees you according to the image of His Son. This is because Christ is your substitute. Christ living in you is actually conforming you into His image. Your past may have been wicked and your present not up to par, but your future is glorious.

You have to quit thinking that you are smarter than God by evaluating yourself, and instead embrace his evaluation: you are His beloved. Some people accept the idea of being loved by God but they translate it in their heads to mean, "God loves a worm like me." That is not what God has in mind. Your faith in Christ restores you to the pinnacle of creation where God created you. You are His workmanship, His handiwork. He loves you as He loves Christ, his Son. You need to repent of agreeing with what Satan thinks of you and embrace what God thinks about you. God says if you are in Christ, you are a new creation, His beloved. (2 Cor. 5:17)

CONFRONTING PRIDE

The hard truth is that every method of significance apart from Christ is ultimately based in pride. If you succeed, you feel great about yourself, and if you fail, you feel horrible about yourself. But regardless, you're trying to value yourself in what you are apart from Christ – a foundation of quicksand. To break the pride cycle, you must become God-conscious instead of self-conscious. When your thought life includes lots of "I, me, and my," you are doomed to pride as well as a host of other sins. Your thought life can be changed and filled with awareness of God's love for you and your love for others.

Jesus was the greatest of all, and He never impressed anyone. In fact, the important people of Jesus' time were pretty unimpressed with Him. Herod laughed at Him like a clown. The only people who esteemed Jesus were those who themselves were not esteemed. So as long as you are chasing the esteem of others, you are chasing the whirlwind. As a follower of Christ, you should never expect to be accepted by the world. In fact, Jesus promises the world will reject you (John 15:19). If you value yourself based on what others think, your life will be run by the fear of man. You will be cool in the eyes of your contemporaries, but your impact will be limited because you are a slave to others' opinions, which are in turn confined by things everyone approves. In order to be influential for God, you have to be able and willing to say the kinds of things others will reject because they are true. This is how it was for every prophet right down to Jesus Himself.

Eliminating pride means becoming ok with who you really are and letting others know that you are ok with it. If you want to get rid of self-consciousness, you have to stop trying to impress other people and believe what God says about who you are. The  feelings of insignificance inside your heart will drive every kind of prideful behavior. The need to be cool, keep up appearances, build a great career or big ministry – all of these things flow from a deep inner sense of insecurity and insignificance. Until you cut out the root of the problem, you will not be able to break the pride on top of it. Whether is it self-exalting or self-abasing, you will not be free until you repent and believe what God says about you. When you believe the truth, the need to "be something" comes to an end.

Don't Be a Punching Bag

Breaking free from the grip of sin includes both what you choose to do and what you to allow to be done to you. You are not a prisoner of fate to others. You have real choices. Real Christianity is unique from most of the world's religions and philosophies because, beginning with salvation, it empowers the individual to make choices which change his or her future. Once you realize your part in the drama, you realize you can change the script. You can end the cycle of victimization in your life.

In many cases, people feel they have "no other choice" to do what they do, but this is rarely true. Most people have a choice between continuing in a negative circumstance and taking an action which may have a cost or be scary. The fear or the cost of the choice makes it seem like there is no choice, but there is. In these situations many people simply opt to continue their negative situation rather than risk what may happen if they change it. For example, when my wife and I wanted to move from Boston to Cincinnati, the housing market was at almost rock bottom and we were poised to lose tens of thousands of dollars. We felt trapped because we desperately wanted to move on with life but did not want substantial loss. For a while, circumstances made us feel we had "no other choice" but to stay. As time went on, however, we realized we still had a real choice. Which was worth more: the money, or moving on with life? When put that way, the choice was easy. We took the loss and moved on. Sometimes choices are hard, but they are always there.

You can see the same pattern with abuse victims who often feel they have no other choice but to stay. But in reality, they make the choice each day to stay and suffer the consequences, rather than take the risk to leave. While the appropriate choice to make here is hard, it is a real one. In many of these cases, it is actually better to risk your life to leave than to stay indefinitely. Carolyn Jessop, author of the best selling book *Escape*, made just such a decision. Faced with a bleak future for not only herself but also her nine children, she decided that rather than be a lifelong slave in a fundamentalist Mormon cult, she would risk everything to be free. At the time she had no money, no resources, one handicapped child requiring hospitalization, and one older child refusing to go. She also had the police department against her, chasing after her and prosecuting her every move. All her friends around her in the same situation said to themselves, "I'm staying for my children." But she was able to realize that "staying for the children" was to curse them with a dark future. It was better to take them and risk it all. This was a hard choice, but the important thing was she realized she actually had a choice.

> "Turn the other cheek" does not mean allowing others to do anything they want to you. It means to keep loving in response to evil.

Intercepting abuse is important because when you keep allowing someone to sin against you, in a twisted way you are helping them to sin. If you take $20 from my wallet and I do not confront you, but then I leave the wallet out on the counter a second time and you take it again, I am allowing you to steal from me. I feel horrible, angry and victimized, but I failed to take the basic step to stop you from stealing again. Until I saw this for myself, I spent many years thinking when Jesus said to "turn the other cheek," it essentially required me to be a doormat to every aggressive person I met. "Turn the other cheek" does not mean "allow others to do anything they want to you." It means, "Keep loving in response to evil."

Jesus teaches us to love others, not to submit to their sin. When the attacker comes do your door, do you invite him in and show him around, or do you defend yourself? When others are involved the choice is clear– we will defend those we love from evil. Yet we are somehow convinced we should not defend ourselves from evil. If someone approached you and demanded your wallet, would you simply hand it over if you did not feel threatened? No, because you have a sense of choice. You know you can choose to say no. When people pressure you to do things, they try to take away your sense of choice so you feel you have no other alternatives. You feel victimized like you must "turn the other cheek" and allow people to do anything they want to you over and over again. But taking this passive approach ensures you will become a slave to the first evil person you meet. Jesus commands us not to resist an evil person (Matt 5:39), but this should not be confused with resisting the evil itself. If Jesus intended absolute pacifism then why did He instruct His disciples to buy swords (Luke 22:36) and let them carry them? You are not required to submit to evil, but to resist it, even if you are the victim. The Kingdom of God is at war with evil (2 Cor 10:3-5), but our warfare is waged through loving even those who have taken advantage of us, not by inviting them to abuse us further.

When I start to talk about the responsibility to break free from those sinning against you, it is too easy to hear me as if I am blaming the victim. I want to say emphatically that I am in no way blaming the victims of terrible crimes for the things that were done to them. In fact, one of the sickest parts of abuse is that abusers try to make victims feel that the abuse is "their fault." Abuse, by definition, is never your fault. What you must take responsibility for is ending the abuse. Jesus commands us to live as *His* servant, not the slave to another man's sin. Whether you are a victim of an abusive spouse, cult, or other dangerous situation, you must have the courage to take control of your life. Take it back from people who want to hurt you and those you love.

You may find yourself a prisoner to others not because they are trying to victimize you, but because you are not expressing yourself or acting upon what you believe. This is much more subtle. By not expressing your preferences to others, you ensure that even well-meaning people will overrun them. Perhaps you feel intimidated because others have strong personalities, or perhaps you feel it is safer to not express what you really think. Regardless, when you do not express what you want or take action, someone else will come along and take action for you.

They may speak for you, and you may not like the result. You always have a responsibility to express yourself and act on your preference. When you do not, you cannot blame others who are bold enough to do so.

Some people live their whole lives feeling frustrated by the action of others around them. They have never stepped up to firmly defend and take action themselves. Theirs is a self-made prison. If you are one of these people, you have lots of rules in your head of what you can and can't do, and what you can and can't say. You "can't" just go to the desk and ask for help. You "can't" just drop in and say hello to your neighbor unannounced. You "can't" just go where you want to go or tell people what you really think. These invisible boundaries are rooted in a perversion of the Golden Rule: "I do not like it when others take action, so therefore I will not take action." Or, "I don't like it when other people make me uncomfortable or ask me to do things, therefore I will not make others uncomfortable or ask them to do things."

We forget that taking no action affects others. Loving others does not mean avoiding actions which might affect them. Loving others means taking action that will affect them positively. You may feel by doing nothing you can avoid making a mistake or sinning, yet serving God by its very nature requires you to take action. How can you make disciples and reach lost people if you take no action and no risk? You have to tell people the truth in order to set them free, and this might make them uncomfortable.

In all likelihood, some of those who have affected you most for good began by getting you out of your comfort zone. Jesus built His ministry around doing things He was not allowed to do and saying things He was not allowed to say. He was not concerned about who He would offend. He was concerned about the people He would help. You can become so concerned about breaking invisible boundaries that you live in a straightjacket, feeling powerless to affect your life and future. You become irritated with others who are taking action which affects your life, but you are not taking it yourself! Satan invented this "be passive" rule, not God. Break out of the chains imposed on your life by others and walk to freedom.

Perhaps the most powerful Scripture in the Bible is Philippians 4:13: "I can do all things through Him who strengthens me." In Christ you have the authority and responsibility to end the "I cannot" and move over to "I can." "I cannot" is simply a prison cell telling you since you cannot escape, you should not even try. You've tried before and it didn't work, so why try again? What is different this time? Almost everyone who ever succeeded in business did so after failing several times. These attempts were not really failures; they were steps on the road to ultimate success. All the great explorers knew just the same thing. They were undaunted by repeated failures because reaching the destination was more important to them than hardships or setbacks.

The truth is, most people give up too easily. They give up at the first sign of real opposition instead of pressing through to victory. Don't let anyone tell you that you can't, or that you just have to wait it out. In Christ you can, and you will.

End Victim Thinking

Escaping the sin of others is one thing, but escaping the pain those sins cause is an entirely different matter. If your own sin was all you had to deal with in this life, that would be hard enough. But unfortunately, you have to deal with the sins of others and the consequences of their sin in your life. When someone sins against you, it leaves a wound in your heart. The hurt comes not primarily from what they actually do, but from the intention behind it. It is the other person's lack of concern or love which hurts the most.

Think of two children on the playground. Billy runs into Jane, and Jane falls down on the ground. When Billy says, "Oh, I'm so sorry, I didn't mean it," and he helps Jane up, she feels better. But when he stands there and laughs, she feels hurt because Billy is saying, "I hurt you on purpose and I liked it." The only way to be healed of these wounds is for the other person to tell us they were sorry, or for us to receive God's love in the place of the other person's cruelty. It is unlikely that those who have wounded us most deeply will ever tell us they are sorry, yet some of us will try to extract an apology from them year after year. When the person who hurt you cannot apologize, you have to turn to God to heal your heart.

Before you can actually receive healing and love from God, you have to make a hard choice— you have to choose to forgive those who hurt you (Matt. 6:15). Some people are terrified of forgiving because they falsely believe forgiveness implies permission for the person to do it again, or a promise of a restored relationship. This is because many abusers use "forgiveness" in just this way. When they say, "Won't you forgive me?" they really mean, "Won't you let me back into your life to take advantage of you again?"

Forgiveness is not what abusive people would have us think it is. It is not permission to be abused again. It is a heart of love toward the person. Forgiveness is releasing the other person from the need to be punished for what they did to you. When you live without forgiveness, you feel a constant need to "make them pay" for what they have done. You replay the wound over and over again until you are filled with anger, even having murderous thoughts toward the other person. Thank God He does not want to "make you pay" for what you have done against Him or others.

If you refuse to forgive, you are the one who suffers, not the person who hurt you. You become a prisoner of the sin they committed against you. While your anger seems to make you feel better about what happened, unforgiveness is your ongoing agreement to be chained forever to the sin. If you stay chained to the sin, you may find that you either become a victim of another abuser or, paradoxically, an abuser yourself. We see this in the cycle of child abuse, for example – most child abusers are themselves former victims.

JUDGMENT

Just like unforgiveness, judgment is a way your thoughts about someone else can ruin your life. The common misconception is when Jesus said, "Do not judge, lest ye be judged," He meant any time you assess anything, you are judging. This leaves you in the impossible position of trying to never evaluate anything. This kind of mindset is actually not Christian at all – it comes from our secular culture where the worst of all sins is to tell someone else they are in sin! Not only did Jesus make very strong evaluations of other people's behavior, the apostles actually rebuked people by name in some of the letters.

What is judgment then? Judgment is the heart of pushing someone else down. God does not see you as your sin, because in Christ, He sees you as forgiven: separate and on the path of separation from your sin. He sees hope for you. Regardless of what evils you have done, He sees your potential. Satan, on the other hand, never stops reminding you of your sin. He does not want you separated from your sin – he wants you to die in your sin.

Judgment, therefore, is when you agree with Satan instead of God about someone else. You say things to others designed to put them down rather than lift them up. You condemn the person instead of helping to separate them from their sin and bring them to life. You know you have entered into a judgment when you think or say things like, "He is a liar" or, "He is a jerk." These are condemning, cursing kinds of statements. They are a prophetic agreement with Satan's plan for the other person. Satan hates other people and he wants to use you to attack them. Ending the cycle begins with loving the other person and having a merciful heart. Coming to the place where you can separate the person from the behavior is an important component. Even if the person lied to you, by labeling them "a liar" you are launching an accusation against their character and identity. This is un-loving. It is designed to push the other person down while lifting you up. It is a human being just like you who told you a lie.

No one we worked with in recovery ministry would have had any hope if we always thought of them according to their sin. In fact, none of us would. We don't see gang bangers, street people, and addicts. We see evangelists, pastors, and worship leaders. We must release people from their sin and see them with the heart of Christ. We have to learn to love other people as Christ loved us. Jesus hated our sin, but He loved us. Loving a person means seeing what is good about them. It means believing good for their future. It means placing value on them as a human being. By choosing to love them in your heart, you experience the positive side emotions associated with having love in your heart. When you judge, the opposite happens: your negative thoughts about others chain you to them and to the negative thoughts. As you curse others, you become cursed.

Judgment, when left unchecked, can reach the point of being what the Bible calls "vain imaginations." Your view of other people becomes completely skewed. You are only able to see the negative things about them, and those negative things are therefore blown out of proportion. Someone gets angry with you one time and you label them an "angry person." Someone takes a Coke from your refrigerator and you label them a thief.

Some people even use the Sermon on the Mount as backup for this kind of thinking. Because Bob got angry with me that means, according to Jesus, he is guilty of murder. Because Bill took my Coke, that means he is a thief. The Sermon on the Mount was designed for you to examine yourself, not to accuse others! Jesus teaches that we are all murderers, liars, thieves, and adulterers by God's standards. If you are seriously going to apply the strict standards of the Sermon on the Mount to others, you should apply them to yourself first. That means if you have ever been angry you need to be given the death penalty for murder. If you have lusted, you need to be stoned for adultery. Are you ready to live up to these standards? The Sermon on the Mount is not a lever to condemn people for their thoughts or minor actions. It is revelation of your own need for mercy and your need to show mercy to others who are also in need of it.

Having mercy means not only having a heart of love and redemption toward the person, it also means seeing a person's actions in the proper context and scale. Deciding to love someone in spite of the fact that you think they are a mean, horrible, evil, deceitful person is not really ending the judgment cycle. It's like saying, "You're worse than Adolf Hitler but I love you anyway." Of course we are commanded to love no matter how bad the person is, but real love not only forgives, it sees the person at the correct scale in the first place. Rarely is the person you are dealing with as bad as your judgments make them out to be. Ok, they get angry at you once in a while. They need to overcome it. That is a long distance from them being the raging tyrant your judgments have made them out to be. Taking your Coke without permission requires confrontation, but it is a long way from being a scheming kleptomaniac.

Another kind of vain imagination is hyper-sensitivity. You become hyper-sensitive to things others do and you interpret all of these actions as though they were attacks against you. For example, if someone seems impatient you might think they are being disrespectful because you have already judged them as being disrespectful and are now building a case against them.

You begin to see every action of others as designed to hurt you. To be frank, most people are not that interested in you. They are just like you – trying to get through life and unable to stay perfectly even keeled all the time. You have to have grace on them, to let them be human. Judgments cause you to perceive all kinds of hurtful things which never really happen. Are you fighting an imaginary war?

REJECTION

Rejection is perhaps the deepest and most lasting pain any one of us carries through life. Yet it is impossible to go through life without experiencing rejection. The only thing that makes each person different is how much you have experienced and how you deal with it. Some people have experienced wounds of rejection in the deepest places. You may feel rejected by parents who abandoned you, by step-parents who hated you, by peers who mocked you, and by lovers who dumped you.

It is natural to internalize these experiences deeply and allow them to tell you something negative about yourself. Then when these people or others try to give you love, you are unable to receive it. You reject yourself in advance so others will not reject you. You make jokes against yourself so others cannot joke against you. You abandon others so they cannot abandon you. You refuse to trust, because someone might break that trust. In other words, you set yourself on an island where you take no risks, so you can experience no pain. This does not protect you from pain though. In fact, it makes you a prisoner of the pain you have stuffed deep inside.

God can heal even the deepest wounds of rejection in your heart, but you will have to learn to be vulnerable. It is amazing how those who have been rejected are continually attracted to people who will reject them again. You are attracted to self-assured people who will tell you exactly what you need to do to please them. You think if you can do exactly what they say, you will be safe and accepted. In reality, it never works like this, because the kind of person who values you for what you do is exactly the kind of person who will reject you.

Real acceptance comes from people who love you regardless of what you do. Sadly, to someone with deep rejection, people who love you for who you are can be scary. They are scary because they do not tell you what you need to "do" in order to be accepted. They ask you to take off your mask and be real in order to have a relationship, and this terrifies a rejected person because it means risking rejection. God Himself is like this, which may be why some people keep Him locked out of the deepest places of their hearts. You may be convinced He is like everyone else and will reject you if you do not perform. Opening your heart to God's perfect acceptance is the first step, and the second step is to find people who love you for who you are and get real with them.

Experiences of rejection can be very real and very painful, but sometimes rejection is actually an invention of your mind. You do not see all of the accepting things people do toward you, you only see the rejecting ones. When you step back to look at the situation rationally it does not really make sense. You're convinced the people around you are rejecting you, yet if they were truly rejecting you, they would no longer be around – they would have left! This happens because you make a decision in your heart that says, essentially, "If this person does not do exactly what I expect them to do, then I am rejected."

Here is a simple example. My wife and I both work in the home. Throughout the day, when we have time, we approach one another to talk. The thing is, when one of us is ready to share, the other person is not. When I greet her and she is busy, I feel rejected. But it is not real — she does not actually reject me. She loves me, she lives in my house and raises my kids, and generally thinks nice things about me. But because she was not ready to talk when I was, I feel rejected. Or perhaps it's an idea you have. You have a great vision for how things should be, but when you present it, other people are not as excited as you are. Does this mean they actually reject you or even reject your idea? No, it may only mean the idea is new to them and they would need to be convinced. Because people do not respond the way you would want them to, you decide you are rejected, but it doesn't match reality.

You have to begin to see the reality of the situation. Does someone truly reject you, or have you decided because they do not react the way you want them to, that you do not fit in? In the case of my wife, she sends me signals both in the small things she does and in the overall orientation of her life, which tell me at the most fundamental level she accepts me. It is upon me to receive and internalize that. It's not her job to start a fireworks display every time I say "hello," in order to convince me of her love. It's my job to see the acceptance she gives in the way she gives it. If I still feel rejected, it is not because she is rejecting me; it is because I have decided that whenever I do not get what I expect, I am rejected.

Rejection can be created through your behavior too. If you start in a lifestyle of sin, those who love you will try to stop you. You have a choice to either hear them and repent, or continue in this lifestyle. When you ignore them, they are forced to take action which you may feel is personally rejecting, but in reality they are rejecting your sin. For example, you were smoking out in your bedroom and refused to stop, so your parents threw you out of the house. You felt rejected, but the rejection was really a result of your own behavior. Most likely those who did it loved you, but could not separate you from your sin. By saying, "If you reject my sin, you reject me," you forced them to reject you.

THE GLASS HALF FULL

One of the things that has amazed me as a father is that the happiness of my children actually has little correlation to the outward circumstances of their life. In fact, if children get what they want all of the time, they become *less* happy. The same could be said when you compare the American lifestyle to those in developing countries. One would think that living in such difficult conditions on the edge of survival would make everyone miserable, yet on the whole, people in these situations are often just as happy as we are – sometimes happier. It's not the outward circumstances but the inner interpretation of those circumstances that give them meaning.

As a military wife, my grandmother would often receive calls from other military wives when they were going to be transferred to the base where she was located. Usually the woman on the other end of the phone would ask, "How is it there?" To which my grandmother would respond, "How is it where you are?" If the woman on the other end of the phone told a story about how miserable things were where she was, my grandmother would tell her that things were miserable in the new location. If the woman told her that things were great where she was, my grandmother would tell her that things would be great in the new location as well. Having lived in places as different as Japan, Guam, Hawaii, South Dakota, and Virginia, she had learned that outward circumstances were not the determining factor of happiness, but the inward attitudes of the heart were.

Because you live in a sinful world, things cannot be perfect all of the time – in fact they rarely are. Like me, you probably don't live in the perfect house or drive a perfect car. You probably don't have perfect friends. Things probably don't go exactly the way you want them to in the mornings. And like me, your bank account probably doesn't have as much money as you would like it to have. People certainly do not treat you in the perfect way either. In other words, at every stage in your life, you have the opportunity to become depressed about something negative.

Take a look at the ancient Israelites. Of course they were miserable in slave conditions, but what is shocking is that when they made it out into the desert, they were unthankful. They did not say to themselves, "Wow, no matter what happens from here, at least we are no longer slaves." Instead they found a reason to complain at almost every point of the journey. They complained about Moses delivering them (Ex. 5:8). They complained about bitter waters (Ex. 15:24). They complained about lack of food (Ex. 16:2) and then when God supernaturally provided it, they complained about that (Num. 21:5). Perhaps greatest of all, when the spies came back to say that the land God was giving them was incredibly fruitful, flowing with milk and honey, they complained that the people in the land would be too hard to conquer (Num. 14:1-4). They actually decided to elect a new leader and go back to slavery in Egypt! Regardless of how God blessed them, the Israelites had decided in their hearts that the glass was half empty.

Even when God came through with a miracle, they still were not thankful. A whole generation had to die in the wilderness because they refused to see and be thankful for what God was doing.

If you are born again, you have something in your life which is to be prized above all things. We learn in 2 Peter 3:7 that the earth and things of this world will eventually be consumed by fire. They are passing away. Even if everything I own were to be stripped from me, I would still be a fabulously wealthy man. I have found the pearl of infinite worth – eternity with God. God has delivered me from eternal fire which I deserve, and into an eternity of loving relationship with Him. It's hard to even comprehend the magnitude of forgiveness and love God has shown to me. To even consider weighing that against something I lack in this life is both absurd and insulting to God.

In the lowest points of my life, I always remind myself of this fact – I am a child of God and no one can take that from me. It is then that I have real perspective. The coveting for more "stuff" ends when you begin to place value on the eternal things: your relationship with God, your relationship with others, especially bringing eternal life to others who would otherwise die without it. When you get to the place where gratitude for your salvation trumps any sense of lack you have in this life, you will be surprised how much better your life is. Nothing has changed, except you have taken on God's perspective.

This perspective is the bedrock of a happy life. On top of it, you must make decisions about everything in your life to see the glass half full. You got in a car accident and it cost you $5000, but thank God they didn't sue you. Or they sued you but thank God you survived the accident which could have cost you your life. You had a hard morning at work, but thank God you have a job at all. Your dinner was not cooked properly, but thank God you had dinner at all. Whatever it is you wish you had better, someone in this world wishes they had had it at all.

It would be nice if you had better stuff and more money. It would be nice if you had an unlimited number of wonderful friends and a spouse who gave you only love all the time. That is just not the way life is, though. You are not perfect, and neither is anyone else around you. You will not ever have the perfect experience. As long as you are playing the script of what you do not have, you will be miserable. Take stock of what you do have and begin to thank God for all of it.

This is hard to see, but it is equally true in relationships. You wish your dad was warmer, but thank God you have a dad. You wish you had more friends, but thank God you have the ones you do have. You wish your spouse were easier to get along with, but thank God you have a spouse. You'll begin to see things rightly when you put them in context to what you could have instead. I promise you, if you think your situation is bad, there is someone else with a situation far worse. If by some chance you have the absolute worst life possible, and have nothing at all but Jesus, you would still have more than millions of people on this planet. Once your relationship with Jesus is your source of joy, everything else gets put into perspective.

I'm not saying you need to rejoice in what is bad or that you should not try to change it. I'm also not saying God is trying to make you love your misery. If two thousand years of gospel history teaches us anything, it teaches us that God likes to alleviate human misery and to bless his children. Your faith can and should be used to break the power of oppressive situations in your life, to walk freely of every hindrance. What I am saying is that no matter if things get better for you or not, happiness begins with being able to see what is good and rejoice in that. If you are not inwardly happy with what you have, you will not be inwardly happy with more.

What attitudes like unforgiveness, judgment, rejection, and ingratitude have in common is they are all ways your own thoughts imprison you. They seem like issues beyond your control which others have to deal with, but in reality you have control of what you choose to think and feel about the situation. Once you break the way you think, you will break free of the pain your thoughts are causing you.

~ Part II ~

Choose God

Take Responsibility

Hopefully in Part I of this book you started see how avoiding responsibility is at the root of bondage. This section is about making the hard choice to take responsibility in every area of your life and surrender to God. When you avoid responsibility it is like permissions slips for sin and Satan to operate in your life. Every time you make an excuse for something, you are giving permission for the problem and consequences to stay. When the smoke from all these excuses clears, your problem is not about anyone or anything else. It's about you and your relationship with God. Once you realize this, you are ready to start dealing with the real root cause of every difficulty— sin. Until you get to this point, I assure you nothing is going to work for you. But once you do, watch out!

People fear taking responsibility because it might make them look bad. And it is certainly true that in the world's system, it is better not to get caught. This game of "cover up" only lasts so long before it comes back to bite you. Think of the politicians who hide their sin in order to stay in power only to be exposed and removed in an instant. Making excuses may keep you from looking bad, but only temporarily. Moreover, which is better: looking bad or actually being bad? If you want to be different, it starts with taking responsibility.

People also fear taking responsibility because instead of seeing a path to freedom, they hear accusation from Satan and others. As they stop making excuses for the problems in their lives, and owning up to their mistakes, they feel condemned. We have a striking visual example of how this works through public shooting sprees and murder-suicides: when the shooter is done lashing out at others, they turn the gun on themselves. This is exactly how Satan works. When you stop blaming others, then he will begin to accuse and blame you. Suddenly when people are told they have responsibility in a situation, they reframe the discussion and say things like, "So you are blaming me?" Taking responsibility is not the same as blame. You have stop giving blame to others for your sin, but you also have to stop taking blame for others' sin on yourself.

Fear of responsibility tends to exaggerate the difficulty of taking it. Blame is about finding a culprit, but responsibility is about finding a way out no matter whose fault it is. Taking responsibility is good news, not bad news. Once you realize what you are doing to contribute to the problem, you have options to overcome it. That's why the blame game ultimately is about Satan's strategy to keep you from getting out. Blame keeps freedom dependent on others' moves; as long as they don't change, you never will. Responsibility opens up what your own moves are.

> **Responsibility is about finding a way out, no matter whose fault it is.**

Freedom begins when the excuses end. Did you do what Jesus, the perfect man, would have done? If not, then you need to accept responsibility for what you did instead. By accepting responsibility, you can begin to change. In reality, there is no excuse for what you have done wrong. Others may have contributed, they may have even pushed you to the edge, but you had to actually jump. Accepting responsibility is what leads you to the Cross. When you own what you have done wrong, you see your need for a Savior. You can give your sin to Him, and receive forgiveness. You can't receive forgiveness for something you do not admit to doing.

Until you accept your sinfulness, you're not really coming to the Cross—you're hiding from it. Modern Christian teaching is light on this point, but recognizing your sin is a message of hope. Once you take ownership for your sin, you can come to the Cross and be changed. Those who claim to be ok cannot receive the transforming power of God. "Good people" have no part in God (Matt. 2:17). You can receive prayer a hundred times at the altar and have no change until you are done being "good" and having excuses for times when you do not act that way.

But for people who see the evil of their sin and want out, there is a river of life which will carry you to freedom. When you admit your sin, God removes it, and you are changed forever by the power of God. When you start to see it this way, sin takes on a new light. You think hiding your sin will protect you, but really you are hurting yourself by hiding it. You are justifying yourself with all kinds of excuses, but these excuses do nothing other than prevent the Cross from working in your life. You need to bring it all out in the open so God can remove it.

I DON'T UNDERSTAND

When you get to the point where you realize you have real problems in your heart, what do you do? You have a choice. You can go back to covering them and managing them, or you can decide you are ready to turn them over to God. This means confronting them and making a hard choice. Many people, once they realize the problem starts with them, try to run from or drown it. This simply avoids the issue while the clock runs out on your life. Freedom means facing the issue head on and deciding you would rather have God than stay the same.

The truth itself is simple but when it meets the web that sin has created in your mind, you experience confusion. When you encounter the truth, you choose whether you will follow it into the light or not. If you choose to respond to truth, more answers become clear. You cannot see what the world would look like from the perspective of truth until you obey God and step into that reality. Further explanation is not what is needed. What is needed is for you to respond to the truth. You can get the truth served up from all kinds of angles using elaborate analogies, but until you are ready to walk and be changed by it, you will end up confused.

When someone confronts you with the truth and you say things like, "I can't see it," or, "I'm not mature enough to do that," or, "I don't understand," this usually shows you are not really hungry for truth. You can see this pattern in John 8. Jesus tells the people they will know the truth, and the truth will set them free. Do the people hear and respond by walking toward freedom? No. They experience confusion saying, "What do you mean? We are already free." Later, the Pharisees asked Him who He was and Jesus said, "Just what I have been telling you from the beginning." In these examples, the people were not looking for truth so Jesus didn't provide any more information. He confronts them with the real problem: "Why do you not understand what I say? It is because you cannot bear to hear my word" (v.43). Their confusion and lack of understanding was not because they lacked information. It was because they failed to believe the information they had already been given. The Son of God was there speaking to them in person, yet instead of submitting to His truth, they opened up a myriad of questions.

Contrast this to the Canaanite woman in Matthew 15 who came in need of a miracle. Jesus first told her that He was "sent only to the lost sheep of Israel," and then, "It is not right to take the children's bread and throw it to the dogs." Now these responses would have easily confused most of us, but the Canaanite woman was absolutely unfazed. She knew Jesus was the Son of God and that whatever He said must be true. She also knew He could and would heal her daughter if she obeyed. She accepted His word, responded in faith, and got the immediate healing she was looking for.

The reason many of us do not have the immediate change we are looking for is not because we lack information – more and more information will make you a good debater but it will not change you. The confusing questions melt away when you respond to the simple truth. Take, for example, the confusion that many people experience when debating "how far is too far" to go with someone who is not your spouse. Debates about the meaning of the words, "adultery," "fornication," and even the Greek *porneia* may ensue, but these debates only exist because human desire is in conflict with the plain teaching of the Word of God. It is easy to see that God's answer to the desire for physical pleasure is marriage. If the simple answer confuses you, it is only because it is in conflict with what you want to do. You're confused because you're suppressing the truth, even subconsciously, and looking for an alternative that cannot be found.

So if you are confused, is it really because you lack information, or is it because you are suppressing the truth? People who really want the truth will run with it when it's given to them. Their minds are not clouded because the Word of God makes plain what they need to believe, and they want to take action when it is explained to them. You can see this in the attitude of the Ethiopian eunuch in Acts 8. He was initially confused by the book of Isaiah and asked Phillip to tell him what it meant. When Phillip explained the passage to him, the eunuch experienced no further confusion. He immediately asked to be baptized. He took action on the truth he was given, which led to salvation and more truth. A person who really wants the truth may need further guidance but only because they are working hard to be changed by the truth they have already received.

Are you looking for an answer when one has already been given? If you have the answer, then it is now on you to repent, act, and believe. You do not need more explanations or questions answered. It is the evil one who brings the endless questions. Questions are only doubts with question marks at the end. You must decide to silence the questions because they are no longer relevant when you believe the truth. When you take the step of faith to believe the plain truth of God's Word, you will be amazed as your confusion simply vaporizes.

> Endless questions are only doubts with question marks at the end.

God or Entertainment?

If pride covers the problem, and blaming passes off the problem, then entertainment medicates the problem. We live in a world and time that is absolutely deluged by entertainment and distraction options. There is always something to do. We do not realize how much things have changed in this way over the centuries. The economic development of Western society has allowed us leisure time like no other point in history. We have vast amounts of time to do whatever we would like to do, and so we have invented a wide variety of ways to distract ourselves from the things which really matter. We have been separated from the gravity of life.

In most of history, for example, death was a very real fact that could occur at any time to anyone. If you got sick, you might be sick for months, you might be sick for life, or you might die from it. People did not expect to live a long life. Now death is something far off that happens to your great-grandmother while she is alone in a hospice. We have forgotten that death and the eternal questions are much more real than our entertainment lives. In fact, we have even invented virtual worlds where you can die and kill repeatedly but never actually die. Death is not real to us.

The impact of all this is that instead of turning to face the problems in your life, you turn to all the other options available. Legendary mathematician Blaise Pascal said it this way: "Nothing is so insufferable to man as to be completely at rest, without passions, without business, without diversion, without study. He then feels his nothingness, his forlornness, his insufficiency, his dependence, his weakness, his emptiness." When the music stops, can you live with yourself?

Entertainment, busyness, and excitement have a purpose in your life – to keep you from wrestling with the things that really matter. In our culture, this can take a thousand forms which we falsely believe give our lives meaning. It could be television and movies, where you can lead a vicarious life through the characters. It could be video games where you can stay occupied for hours on end while playing God, never dying, and never having to interact with another human being. It could be sports, where you can have meaning and value because of someone else's achievements. It can be shopping, where the rush of having something new generates excitement in your life. It can be the internet, where anything you could ever want to know, or anyone you could want to meet are right at your fingertips. It could be art, music, collecting, traveling, or an esoteric hobby which provides a challenge and journey for you. It could even be something that has a legitimate role in your life – your work, family, church, or other important service. It does not really matter what your diversion of choice is, it matters that you have been distracted from facing your problems head on, from growing in God, and most importantly, from helping others.

One way people distract themselves is through unnecessary activities. These things may seem good or necessary, but they are really just distraction. They are invented to avoid the real priorities. I see this a lot with people who cannot stay in one place. If things are not going well in life, the answer becomes "go, go, go!" You don't know where you are going or why you are going, but you are going. You run from city to city, job to job, but as the old adage goes, "Wherever you go, there you are." When the opportunity to get face to face with God arises, or to meet a counselor who wants to help, suddenly it is time to replace the heater that has been broken for five years.

The problem is that you cannot get away from yourself. You will follow yourself everywhere you go. You think you are running from others and the situations they put you in, but really you are trying to get away from you. It is your character that put you in the situation you are in. There are great things to be said for those who take action, but not when the action is a substitute for taking the *right* action. Do you find yourself going from one pursuit to the next, or from one task to another? It's probably because you are searching for fulfillment, running from yourself, or running from God.

It's not surprising. Our culture conditions children from birth that life is all about excitement. We feel we have wronged our children if we have not given them the most sugary treats, shown them the most popular videos, taken them to the most exciting amusement parks, and given them the most cool games and opportunities. They are children; they are supposed to have fun, right? This teaches them, however, that life is all about thrill and excitement. We wonder why they become addicted to drugs and other things later when they are supposed to be working or otherwise being responsible. It should come as no surprise because they have already been taught to be addicts.

In some sense, drugs are the greatest form of entertainment of all. The thrill and excitement of a chemical high keep you coming back for more. When someone comes off of meth, one of the most common complaints is they are "bored." Nothing in real life seems to match the excitement that being high for days gives you. The process of living life feels so banal and uninteresting. But it isn't life which needs to change; it is you.

Like many young men of my generation, I spent seemingly endless hours growing up on video games. In my case, they were 'god games' where I could control and run my own virtual world. I thought there was nothing wrong with it, but as I sought the real God, He told me I had a choice – I could either have meaning in a virtual life or meaning in my real life. That settled it for me – I wanted a real life, not a virtual one. Similarly, some people are addicted to the news. Do you want to read the news or make the news? Which life do you want? You can spend your time in an imaginary world and the rewards will be imaginary, or you can spend your time in the real world and the rewards will be real.

THRILLED BY GOD?

We bring this thrill addiction over into our expectations of God and church. We want it to be exciting and entertaining more than we want it to be transforming. We go to church looking for the best music, the biggest name, or the most exciting teachings. We like it if it's hyped up. If it's larger than life, we want to be there. We believe an exciting program is going to help us meet God more, so we want fireworks and we want them now.

There are different ways this comes in the door, but at the root, they are all manifestations of the same problem. The most obvious way this happens is when we turn church into a production that is focused on attracting and holding people. Sometimes we do this under the banner of being "seeker-friendly." Jesus was friendly to seekers but there was certainly no show. Are you going to church to be entertained?

Church can become a show for spiritual reasons too. I remember going to a service with one of the nation's most well known evangelists. In Boston, where we were living at the time, it is hard to get a thousand Christians together to do anything, but this evangelist was easily able to pack out the Garden for several nights. I went with an open mind to find out what was going on. Several "miracles" took place, but they were all carefully and obviously choreographed, including ministers on the stage falling over when cued, and a parade of people bringing a wheelchair forward. The miraculous had been turned into a show. The ministers on the platform who fell on cue probably even believed it was ok because it would "build up people's faith." People were so hungry for it, they were willing to ignore the obvious signs that it was scripted, not the moving of the Holy Spirit. Hype and excitement are so seductive that many would simply rather ignore the truth to keep the show going.

This happens even in parts of the church that do not believe in faking it. We will go from one conference to another looking for the power encounter because we think Christianity works better when it's dramatic. That's they way I used to be. I've had some exciting experiences with God, but what happens in between those times? Do I need to keep running from meeting to meeting, looking for another one? I started to realize it is the times "in between" that are actually the main event. The main event is heaven in my heart, every hour of every day. The main event is bringing heaven to others. Fulfillment begins when you let go of the need to be excited and you embrace the need to be changed. Are you expecting God to do for you what the fallen world does for you, but only better? Are you trying to "get high" from God? If so, you've just baptized addiction. What God does to you won't be like what the world does, but it will be more fulfilling. He won't feed a "high" every day. He will help you embrace the changes you need to happen inside. When you let go of the need to be thrilled you will start on the path to stability.

> Your feelings do not indicate what is true, they indicate what you believe.

Maybe you are going to meetings to get a feeling. Maybe you want an encounter which will convince your heart of something you doubt. You lack joy, conviction, assurance, or something else and are hoping a meeting or experience will fix it. The problem is that this is backwards. Your feelings do not indicate what is true; they indicate what you believe. For example, maybe you doubt that you are saved, so you feel depressed. You really are saved, but you want an experience to remove your depression. Your depression will go away only when you stop doubting your salvation. No emotional meeting will stave the doubts off forever.

Feelings are important indicators of what is going on in your life, so I am not saying to ignore them – I am saying you cannot chase them or determine truth from them. Instead you must find out what is underneath those feelings and change them to be in line with the truth. As you change your heart and life to be in line with the truth of God, your feelings come into line. An emotionally stirring meeting can make you feel better for a while, but changing your heart will make you feel better permanently.

Even conservative segments of the church are in on the act. Under the banner of "Christian hedonism" we have been told that instead of dying to the selfish pursuit of pleasure, you can just redirect it toward God. God's greater pleasure is supposed to trump the pleasures of this world. This misses the mark for two reasons. First, it teaches us that our pleasure is the center of our relationship with God. Secondly, it fails to confront worldly expectations about pleasure. Christianity is not about a selfish pursuit of anything.

In fact, by itself, even experiencing God in deep ways does not cure the excitement addiction. There is no doubt that ministering under the power of God is the greatest rush known to man, but if you are focused on the rush, then you will feed the addictive personality even as you do mighty things in God. Great ministries have fallen for just this reason. They got to the place where they needed a "God fix" and when they couldn't get enough they started turning to something else to feed the addiction. Should you bring faith and expectation to a meeting when you approach God? Absolutely. But what are faith and expectation for? Emotional relief? Or to see a miracle? That is what king Herod wanted out of Jesus – he had Jesus brought before him because he was hoping to see a sign (Luke 23:8). That was the extent of his interest. Your faith and expectation should be around God coming close to His people and His people coming close to Him.

END THE ADDICTION

Excitement addiction is cured when what thrills you, changes. 1 Corinthians 13 teaches us that miracles, words of knowledge, and every other exciting thing will cease, but love will never cease. Love is therefore what you should pursue. It is eternal and non-addictive. It is the goal of all of the activity of the Holy Spirit. Nothing you can dream of can touch the transforming love of God. There are deep waters in relationship with Him.

The pleasure of knowing God is in fulfillment, not excitement. Jesus even told the disciples not to rejoice that demons submitted to them, but to rejoice in their salvation (Lk. 10:17-18). Having real relationships where you have love deep in your heart is the greatest pleasure on earth, and the eternal relationship with God is the greatest of all. It is the gift that keeps on giving. Deliverance from sin and death is the fulfillment that never wanes. In the world you are chasing something, but in Christianity, you are in relationship with Someone. This world deals in thrills but God deals in life transformation and relationships.

Life is not about excitement and fun. The person who is chasing these things will always be a slave to the next high of whatever their choice diversion is. Excitement and fun are substitutes for real life and loving relationships. Excitement and fun are substitutes for the deep sense of purpose which comes from giving your life completely over to God and helping other people. Excitement is the carrot on the stick that keeps you enslaved. It does not matter what your drug of choice is; Jesus says, "Everyone who sins is a slave to sin" (John 8:34)

It's not just exciting things like fame, fortune, and success that can be addictive either. Some people get their fix from things which seem completely undesirable: control, anger, mistrust, self-isolation, depression, anxiety, etc. We worked with a young man who struggled greatly with anger. Every month or so he would go on a multi-day binge of being angry. Finally we told him he would have to choose to repent of anger or choose to move out. We told him we would help him overcome the anger, but he would have to make the choice to die to it and start fighting with us instead of against us. It was a hard choice because he realized the anger was a friend to him, which made him feel better in some way. However, once he realized this, he made the right choice. The undesirable sins exist because at some level we actually want them. They are familiar and comfortable. They take the edge of a deeper, underlying problem. It's like being addicted to painkillers.

The enjoyment of sin—the pleasure it offers—is the reason you hold onto it. If it offered you no pleasure at all, you would release it. Breaking free means deciding you would rather have God than any thrill or excitement the world could offer. It means you would rather have God than some familiar attitude which offers you solace. It means that at the most fundamental level, you are done seeking your selfish pleasure and are in pursuit what God wants. You want to be rid of *even the craving* for thrill, and you want to step into the deep river of God.

Die to Yourself

Are you ready to come down off the permanent high or do you still want to do it your own way? As long as you have bought into the pleasures of this world, you are a slave to them. Few people are really ready to take the big jump and leave the world behind. They think they are, but when confronted with the area in their lives where they want to be in control, the truth comes out. They are like the rich young man who came to Jesus asking what he must do in order to be saved. When he was told that he must crucify the idol of money in his life by selling everything he had (Matt. 19:16-22), that was it for him. He was done. He wanted the "follow God and keep my idol" option, which was not available. The invitation to follow Jesus is an invitation to come and die. To follow Christ you must deny yourself. This means bringing an end to all of your selfish purposes and embracing God's purposes. You die to your worldly pursuits and find in their place joy and fulfillment that comes from pursuing what is on the Lord's mind: the salvation of the lost, and a deeper relationship with Him.

God does not offer a middle of the road option where you give Him control of most of your life and keep a couple of pet areas for yourself. Most people would be fine with Christianity if there were such an option. "I'll quit smoking, as long as I can run with the same godless friends." "I'll go to church, as long as I can chase girls on the side." Jesus says, "enter through the narrow gate, because wide is the gate and broad is the road that leads to destruction" (Matthew 7:13). Trying to have both God and the world is the broad road of destruction.

Adam's step of eating the fruit was rebellion against the authority of God. He knew what was right and he chose to do it his own way. Sometimes when people encounter God, rebellion goes underground instead of getting dealt with. Rebellion is not just the rejection of what you are supposed to do. Rebellion is in what you feel energized about doing. You were completely energized about sex before you were married, but now that you are married you find sex with your spouse uninteresting. You used to dance the night away and act wild when you were unsaved, but dancing for God is embarrassing. You are completely pumped up about the sports game and will shout at the TV, but you think it is awkward to give a shout for God. When you were in the world, you would have worked like a slave to get to the next rung on the ladder, but you feel dull and bored when thinking of doing things in God's Kingdom. You are pumped about chasing anything your heart desires, but if someone gives you direction, you feel demotivated. The future seemed bright and open when you were on the way to hell, but now that you are walking with God, you feel constricted.

> Rebellion is in what you feel energized about doing.

It's easy to excuse these kinds of feelings by saying you are fallen and the devil is working against you, but really they are signs that you need to change. Having inward passions toward the things of the world while outwardly doing the right thing is living a false life. These feelings are indicators that you have not really surrendered it all to God. You are putting on a veneer to do the right thing, but deep inside your pleasures and interests are still worldly. When you have really given everything over to God, your passions change. You become stirred up by the thought of a soul coming to Christ, not by the thought of the episode of your favorite show. You become hungry for real relationships, not being in the cool crowd. You are internally energized by the things of God, not the next exciting thing.

Cleaning up a little bit on the outside will make your life happier but it will not remedy your fundamental problem – you are a sinner. Very few people actually think of themselves as bad people. You think you are a good person who just hit a few bad breaks. A truly good person like Jesus does not do anything bad. Not only that, a truly good person does not need to be trained or make an effort to do good things. A truly good person does not enjoy sin. When put in those terms it is easy to see that people are not truly good. Your problem is not a few bad breaks or even an occasional sin, it is actually your nature. You are sinful. If it were just a few mistakes, then self-improvement or reform could deal with the issue. If that were enough, however, there would have been no need to put Jesus on the Cross. The Cross is God's declaration of how bad your problem really is. There is no solution to it. It requires death.

In order to be born again, you had to realize and accept this. You were baptized in water to show you died to your old life and everything it offered, so that you could be raised unto a new life with God. Realizing how deep the problem is can be a progressive thing, however. I accepted by faith how bad I was when I was a fairly "good" kid in middle school. It took me more than 15 years of struggling with sin to realize the evil and deceitfulness of my own heart. I became convinced on a much deeper level how much I needed a Savior and how my own human effort was completely inadequate to change me.

Many people interpret the step of dying to self to mean something it is not. Dying to self does not mean trying to loathe everything you love. It does not mean if you like chocolate, then God commands you to eat only vanilla for the rest of your life. It does not mean that if you like Sally, you have to marry Sue. Don't get tricked into thinking God wants whatever you find difficult. It's a lot like how grandmothers always thought cod-liver oil would cure everything because it was so disgusting. Dying to yourself is not about denying yourself things you inwardly prefer. It is realizing your heart wants things that God hates, and deciding you want to turn away from those things, towards Him. It means the orientation of your life changes.

The step of surrendering to God is different than being completely free from sin. If you could come to God free from sin, then you would not need a Savior. Surrender means you are now on God's team against your sin, rather than trying to defend and avoid your sin.

> **Surrender means you are on God's team against your sin, rather than defending or avoiding it.**

Jesus' message in the gospels was not a new and more difficult list of do's and don'ts. It was an impossible list. You absolutely cannot follow the commands of the Sermon on the Mount (Matthew 5-7). Only Jesus living inside of you can. He gave those commands to expose your need for Him. He gave those commands to show you the absolute impossibility of being "good." The harder you try to follow them, the more you realize something is radically wrong.

Coming to the Cross is getting to that point. It is getting to the point where you do not want the world anymore. You know you can't get free from sin on your own but you really do want to. You know you can't be right with God on your own, but you really do want to. You know you are unable to self-reform, and you need the divine power of God to change you.

Many sins are simply manifestations of the fact that you have not yet decided God is going to be first in every area of life. If God is not first, then who or whatever is, is your real god. The orienting factor of your life, where you live, what you do with your time, who you choose to surround yourself with, should be God. That is when He is really first. The core of repentance is the realization that the pleasures of this world are nothing compared with the pleasures of God. The pleasures of this world are short lived, but the pleasures of God are forever. You come seeking ministry with a list of symptoms, but when the spiritual doctor says you must repent and turn away from the pleasures of this world, do you cringe and go off to seek an alternative solution? You have to realize everything you put in front of Him is an obstacle to your happiness anyway. God doesn't hate sin because we enjoy it. He hates it because it hurts us and other people.

Until you put God in charge you will simply be pursuing a band-aid for the root cause of your problem. You are trying to fix your problems without fixing their roots. You must die to the world and live unto God. Your love for money, for sex, for success, for the praise of others, or for the things of this world is an iron chain around your neck. The more you seek the things of this earth to fulfill you, the emptier you will be. And it is not just the exciting things you have to give up, it's every kind of sin.

Death to yourself means deciding to turn away from and stop coddling whatever comforts you apart from God.

Changing means leaving behind the things, and sometimes even the people, you are attached to. Changing means turning away from temporal pleasure and excitement, taking a long view and embracing the peace and fulfillment which comes from loving God. This fulfillment is a freedom worth more than anything the world could ever offer you. This freedom is worth it even if you have to take drastic action. Do you want to deal with the root cause or just keep putting a band-aid on the symptoms?

~ Part III ~

Accept God's Love

The Love of God

God loves you. This seems like such a simple idea, yet it is so hard for most of us to grasp and experience. Because of negative life experiences and emotions, you may feel that God is far away and unconcerned about your well being. You may be convinced that He is either unconcerned, unable to help, or in the worst case, actually wants you to be in pain. If this is the way you think, then you have bought into Satan's plan to separate you from God.

Satan's goal is to convince you that God is like him and he is like God. He wants you to believe God is distant and uncaring, and if possible, mean and vindictive. He knows that as long as you think this way, you will run from God instead of toward Him. When you believe these lies, you give Satan power over you. In essence, by believing God has the character of Satan, you make Satan god of your life. When something bad happens and you ask, "Why God?" this empowers Satan.

When God created the world, He gave authority over it to mankind. He told us to "be fruitful and multiply and fill the earth and subdue it and have dominion," (Gen. 1:28). When Adam and Even listened to the voice of Satan, they gave this authority over to Satan. Ever since then, we have all been born as citizens of his dark kingdom. You are born into it and choose it continually by your sin and beliefs about God. When bad things happen, it is simply a manifestation of Satan's kingdom at work. It is not a manifestation of God's will.

When you get the two reversed you will start to ask yourself questions like "Why do bad things happen to good people?" and not long after that you will be tempted to blame God for your problems. When you remember that sin is the source of evil, and Satan is the one who attacks the righteous, not God, your life will go a lot better. Instead of shadow-boxing God, and experiencing deep emotional turmoil, you can have peace knowing that the creator is for you. And if God is for you, who can be against you? (Rom 8:31)

If you want to know what God's attitude really is toward you, you need to look at Jesus. He was the perfect expression of the Father's character on earth. (John 5:30). Look at his ministry. When He came, He never put sickness or pain on anyone. Not only did He not permit evil in His life, He openly opposed it in the world. He then turned to the disciples and told them to go and make disciples of the whole world – in essence He said, "Go take my Kingdom back. Confront and drive out evil wherever you go." That's God's attitude toward the pain and evil in your life. He wants you to become His disciple and drive it out.

Therefore, the first and most important reason you are not experiencing God's love is not because it is not there, but because you do not really believe in it. As soon as storms or difficulty or negative emotions come back, you start to feel God must not really love you. Think of God's love like the sun – an intensely powerful warmth directed toward you. Doubting God's character is a false belief, a cloud which blocks you from feeling His love.

Take a hug for example. It is not just the experience of the hug that communicates love to me. It is what I believe the hug means to the other person. If someone gives me a hug and I do not think they are sincere, I will not feel any love at all. I might feel used or manipulated, or even angry. All of those emotions are happening on my end of the relationship however! The person who is hugging me feels love toward me, but I do not receive because of my false beliefs about them. It is not because they aren't giving love or feeling it toward me. It is because my false beliefs are leading me to a false interpretation and then a wrong experience of what is really happening. Do you see how this applies to your relationship with God? God is always there sending love toward you,

> If your feelings are telling you that God doesn't love you, your feelings are lying.

but if you do not believe in it, you will never feel it. Before you feel the love of God, you must choose to believe in his loving heart toward you. Only then will you be able to receive His love.

People say they will know God loves them when they "feel it." But this is backwards. You will not feel loved by God until you are absolutely convinced of His love for you. Jesus' death on the Cross is the definitive statement of that love. There is no greater love than to sacrifice your life for someone else. God would die for you – that's how much He loves you. If your feelings are telling you that God doesn't love you, your feelings are lying. When you let pain, suffering, feelings, or other things convince you God does not love you, you are denying the powerful demonstration of love in Jesus' death on the Cross.

Think of God's love is like the sun. The sun burns brightly

day and night regardless of anything we do on earth. There is literally nothing you can do to stop it. Even if it passes behind a cloud, the sun is still there. The clouds are the things you believe and the things you do which put a wall between you and God. His love is always shining down toward you, but you have allowed or even created a barrier which blocks the flow of His love toward you. By accepting these false beliefs about God, you exchange the nature of Satan for the nature of God. You think that God doesn't love you, but the God you are trying to relate to is more like Satan than God! Clear the clouds away, and the warm touch of God's love will flow into you.

You can see this in the famous story of the prodigal son in Luke 15:11-32. A father had a son who rebelled against him, took the inheritance, and spent it on wild living. Many fathers would have completely disowned the son and never spoken to him again. Yet this father was different. After the son decided to return home, Jesus says that "while he was still a long way off, his father saw him and felt compassion, and ran and embraced him and kissed him." This father loved his son so much that he must have had his eyes on the horizon looking for him constantly, hoping the son would appear. When he saw the son, before asking any questions or putting down any conditions, he ran, embraced him, and kissed him. He had been longing to give this lost son his love, and now that the son was home, he did not miss the chance. God is this kind of father. His love is toward you regardless of anything you are doing.

Am I saying God does not care about sin? No. God loving you and you being in right relationship with Him are two different things. The father loved the prodigal son even while he was out spending the inheritance. He hoped the son would come home and restore the relationship, but he loved the son regardless. That's how God feels about you as well. His love is not conditioned on anything you do. Sometimes simply realizing this fact is enough to cause a person to want to come back into right relationship with God.

Look at what the prodigal son says to his father after the father has lavished his love on him: "Father, I have sinned against heaven and before you. I am no longer worthy to be called your son." The son realized he was out of relationship with his father, accepted responsibility, and asked forgiveness. Some people think God's unconditional love means they can live like the devil and be in relationship with God, but this is a fantasy. When you choose a life of sin, you choose a life apart from God. You erect a barrier between yourself and God. That's why sin is the third cloud in the diagram. Choosing a life of sin creates a barrier to you actually experiencing the love of God. The father loved the son while he was far away, but it was not until he came home that the son *experienced* that love. Turning away from sin and toward the love of God are the same thing. You cannot abide in God's love if you are also abiding in sin. You must come into His presence desiring to have sin removed from your life, and He will do it. The more you abide in God's love, the less your appetite and desire is for sin. This is the power of what the Bible calls "grace."

WHAT ABOUT THE REST OF THE BIBLE?

Like many Christians, I used to play "dial-a-verse" with my Bible when I first got started with God. I would look for him to speak to me by opening up to some random page. And more often than not, I would open up to some condemning prophecy in the Old Testament. This was discouraging for me. I wanted to see God as loving but kept being confronted with this really scary stuff. After reading pages and pages of condemnation, it was hard to see God's love through it.

Especially in the years that I was in college trying to pioneer my way through life with what felt like opposition on all sides, I really craved mercy. Can God provide kindness and mercy that is tangible in your life or is it just limited to the theological idea of kindness and mercy? It's one thing to understand abstractly that God is a loving Person, but it is quite a different thing to experience Him that way. It's one thing to know Him as the one who gave you new life, and it's another thing to know Him as the one who is still giving you new life every day.

Eventually I realized something quite simple but easy to miss: the scary verses in the Bible are directed at those who do not want to follow Him. The kind verses are for those who have submitted to Him. Reading the scary verses over and over again and trying to apply them to yourself is like reading someone else's prison sentence. I'm thankful that the government can be hard and forceful with people who do evil things, and I'm thankful that God shows Himself equally strong in opposition to evil. But God reveals Himself to you according to who you are. For those who are attracted to evil, He will reveal Himself as strong and shrewd. For those who want to have a relationship with Him, He wants to reveal Himself as kind and merciful (Psa 18:25).

If you are one who wants to know God with all of your heart, the Bible is a gateway to the limitless kindness and mercy of God. I believe David discovered this when he worshipped God as a shepherd boy. All David had on paper to understand God was the first five books of Moses. There is not a lot of stuff there to warm your coffee mug. Yet, when David began to approach God as one whose first motivation was love, he discovered a fountain that wouldn't run dry. He became the driving force behind the book of Psalms – which is one of the fullest representations of God's love in the Bible. David's faith about God's character took him into a place of relationship with God which exceeded his wildest imagination.

Think about the books of Moses: the Law was given to a people who wanted a way to relate to God from afar – a way that did not require repentance. The Bible says they wanted to relate to God from a safe distance (Exod. 20:19). Yet Moses and Joshua, whose hearts were turned toward God, discovered that relationship with God was something awesome – so awesome that Joshua did not want to leave the tabernacle (Exod. 33:11). The smoke and the fire are warning signs for those who do not want to know God, but for those who do, there is an infinitely deep relationship waiting to be had.

The God of Mercy

For me, simply discovering the verse where God promised to comfort the people of Jerusalem like a "mother" (Isa. 66:13) took away a lot of stress. He is not just the God of power and authority, He is the God of mercy and comfort. In fact, He invented them. Look at any culture that has never been touched by Christianity and you will be hard pressed to find mercy. The ancient Romans thought it was a weakness, but God calls it a virtue. God is the one who remembers that your life has value when no one else does. He is the one who will send a whole nation to war to stop the evil of slavery. The one who will motivate thousands to risk their lives for young girls in the sex trade or for babies who have not been born. He remembers and thinks about every life as precious. God is not a theological idea, sitting far off in the heavens. He is a person who cares about you far beyond what you could ever imagine. He would do anything to have a relationship with you—even die on a Cross.

If you look closer, you will find that a lot of the scary stuff in the Bible was directed at those who refused to show mercy – a lot like the policeman who is there to save you from being mugged. I'm glad to have someone in my corner in a dark and difficult world. If you are broken in life and seeking him humbly, do not be afraid of Him. The Bible says a "bruised reed He will not break" (Isa. 42:3). He doesn't want to wipe you out. He wants to transform you with His love.

When you get down to it, this is really what knowing God is all about – being transformed by His love. Once you begin to see Him through the eyes of love, as the author of love, as the very definition of love, then you have begun to know Him really (1 John 4:8). The more you abide with Him in this way, the more He will soften your heart, so that you see the world through His eyes – the eyes of a God who cares even about a sparrow that falls to the ground.

The fact that God knows the hairs on your head is not simply a statement of His omniscient mind; it is statement of the depth of His interest and concern for you. He is so concerned about you that He knows you're coming in and going out. He knows your thoughts. He knows your interests. He knows your friends and your family. It is a statement about how deep His love really goes, and just as importantly, it's a statement of how deeply you can experience His love when you abide in Him. You need never walk alone again, or feel alone again, or wonder "Why, God?" His heart is always towards those whose heart is towards Him.

Grace

It takes more than knowing that God is loving to change you. You must know His love applies to you specifically. If God is loving in general, but has not forgiven you in particular, then it makes no practical difference. And this is the point where many people struggle. A true understanding of grace is what is needed to break the logjam.

We know from the Bible that we are "saved by grace," but what does this really mean? Grace is God's answer to sin, so it comes as no surprise that a great deal of confusion exists about what grace is really all about. The popular definition of grace is "unmerited favor." And while there is nothing wrong with this definition, it is often used to imply that sin has no impact on your relationship with God, or that the impact it has is only in your head. Grace becomes the reason why God winks at sin after the fact. It becomes an excuse for the sin you cannot overcome – exactly what Paul said he did not teach. (Rom. 6:1)

On the other end of the spectrum, some people actually teach that grace is the reason why you have no excuse for your sin. They like to say, "Grace raises the standard." Now that you are under grace, you're not supposed to even think about sin. You must start fixing it or else! People who define grace this way actually negate the grace of God and turn the New Testament into a new, impossible law. The more you try to obey such a law the more corruption you will feel in your own heart. You will end up right where I was – in terror, or in sin.

These two extremes present an incomplete picture of grace. Grace does not mean that God does not care about sin *or* that He condemns you for not being free. A fuller definition is, "The unmerited favor of God which empowers you to change." When Jesus died on the Cross, He removed the barrier of sin which separated you from the Father. Believing in Him means you accept that you are sinful beyond any self-improvement. You accept that the love of God is a gift given to you based on Jesus rather than what you do. This is not just a fact of salvation, this is actually the way you live the Christian life. It is the love, the approval, and the forgiveness of God abiding in your heart that set you free from sinful behavior.

When you approach God in this way you are saying, "God you were right about me. I do deserve to die. So I am relying on your Son to approach you." You no longer want to keep leading a lifestyle of sin. Grace is only a license to sin for those who want to keep leading the sinful lifestyle. People who are not willing to turn from sin are not really receiving grace. Yet you should not confuse this with having to be fixed before you can approach God. Grace is the ability to approach God without having to present a litany of sins and making sure you have made every one of them right before you approach. Grace is God saying, "I take your sins from you and I give you my love instead, so you'll be changed."

As you turn from sin and towards the love of God given to you without condition, you break sin's grip on your life. This is true grace, and it is what you need to be free. Grace reverses the order of operations with God. First receive His love, and *then* you will be cleansed from sin. Do not try to fix your sin first (the outside of the cup) in order to receive His love (the inside of the cup). God's love for you is unilateral. He gives it, you receive it, and as you receive it, you are released from sin.

This is what the Bible calls living by faith. You get into faith when you stop trying to get significance, acceptance, love, or other fundamental needs met by doing things to please God. You enter into faith when you start receiving these things as a gift. It sounds so simple, yet it confounds our darkened minds. You have to literally learn how to walk by faith. Faith begins when you believe in God's unconditional love for you and His forgiveness through the Cross of Christ. You "walk by faith" when you begin to abide in and meditate on His love in your heart.

The more you meditate on that love and in your closeness to God, the more you become like Him and are able to walk righteously. Freedom from sin happens because you receive His love.

GRACE OF THE MIND

Applying God's grace will transform you to the image of Christ. Some people think more head knowledge about grace will somehow help them to overcome, but you need more than accurate knowledge. What you need is to actually abide in the love of God given to you through Christ. If you receive it and abide in it, you will have the power to overcome sin. As you abide in God's love, you feel His divine empowerment. When you come to God in worship and present yourself, you are changed.

There are many related concepts in the body of Christ which are used to address the same issues as grace. Some emphasize the "finished work" of Christ. They say you need to know more about what Christ did for you in order to be free. In this view, there is nothing additional to do on your part except to know what He did. This phrase "finished work," however, is a bit of a trick. Of course Christ has done it all and you can't add to it. That does not negate the fact that you need to do something to experience the fullness of what Christ finished. If you did not need to do anything at all, you would be doing miracles on your couch while watching *The Simpsons* reruns.

The real question is, what exactly do you need to do in order to walk in the work that Christ finished? "Finished work" teachers may say you don't really believe in the New Covenant, but the real problem is that you don't actually *practice* the new covenant. Walking in the New Covenant is not just what Christ did, it's how you respond to what He did. I am a strong believer in the New Covenant and the new creation in Christ, but these are not realities to just know about. They are realities you step into by actively removing false beliefs within, and allowing the experience of God's love to take you to a higher place.

Similarly, it is often suggested that you have "two natures" and need to walk in the "new nature." This can create a kind of double-mindedness where you think your sin resides in one part of you while the other part of you is perfect. Telling yourself to walk in the new nature and proclaiming you are a "new man" does not address the problem because it ascribes sin to a part of you that you can't change. Only applying God's love and grace to your one whole person will change you. You put the deeds of the flesh to death by the power of receiving God's love.

In the same vein, some believe once they are saved, they cannot possibly lose their salvation. The problem is this leads to a misplacement of faith. Instead of actively placing your faith in Christ, you begin to place your faith in a belief that you can't lose your salvation. It leads you to think back to the moment of your salvation to make sure it really happened. If you are not exactly sure when you were saved, then you begin to wonder if you really were saved. Then you worry that every time you sin you might never have been saved, or that you might have committed the unpardonable sin. Because of this problem, a doctrine which was designed to give security actually denies security to many sincere people. Even worse, it gives a false sense of security to another group of people who have no intention of walking rightly with God. The real security of salvation is not in a doctrine that says you could not possibly lose your salvation, but in your living, active relationship with Christ *now*. You have security because you are abiding in Christ *now*.

These concepts are not fundamentally false. But they put the focus on something you must know rather than on heart transformation. Experiencing freedom is not just about what Christ did; it is about what you do about what Christ did. By that I do not mean you have to behave better, dress holy, or strain out sin – that's living in works. What I mean is that you have to step into the reality of Christ. As your heart becomes more and more deeply like Christ's, and you believe how He believed, you experience more and more of God in your life. You produce the fruit of good deeds, which is very different than pursuing and putting stock in those deeds. So there is unfinished business, not a finished work. You must actively participate by applying the grace of God to your heart.

You must change more than your theological beliefs. You must change your heart. As you allow your heart to be fully persuaded of God's truth at the deepest hidden levels, you experience more of the life of Christ.

Works

The opposite of walking in grace is living in works. Living in works is completely natural and logical to us, but it is also wrong. Works are when you try to perform in order to be loved. You try to clean yourself up so that God will love you. The worst part is, while your outward performance may convince you that you are walking by God's grace, the inner strife tells a different story: you are actually operating in human effort trying to "be right" for God to love you. If you believe that by doing certain religious activities you are in better standing with God, you are in works. If you need to do certain religious activities in order to feel loved by God, you are in works. You believe your human effort has the effect of keeping you right with God. If you have any success in your behavior modification without actually changing your heart level beliefs, then your obedience is only outward.

Works obeys the letter of the law while inwardly desiring to disobey it. Works is a special trap just for those who actually believe in God's law. Jesus addressed it head on with the religious people of His day, saying, "You clean the outside of the cup and the dish, but inside they are full of greed and self-indulgence" (Matt. 23:25). Repentance is what allows you to clean the inside of the cup and dish. Until you repent, it is like trying to hold water back in a leaky dam with your finger – more leaks will keep springing until either you drown or you drain the lake!

Cain was the first one to ever believe in works. He worked hard on the ground God had cursed and then brought an offering to show God what a "good" thing he had done. "God will approve of me because I am good," he thought in his heart. But God could not accept the offering because it was arrogant and false – Cain was not good; he was wicked at heart. His brother Abel knew this was true of himself, which is why he offered the animal sacrifice. Abel thought in his heart, "I am worthy to die, but perhaps God will accept this offering instead of my death."

When you think you are good because of all the good things you do for other people, or for God, you are in works. All born-again Christians profess they are not saved by works, but many still try to become more righteous by human effort. They read their Bible more, pray more, fast more, or do other things to feel like God likes them more. If you are doing that, you are bringing a Cain offering to God. It will make you farther away from God, not closer.

It is amazing how committed Satan is to this way of salvation and self-improvement, and how logical it seems to the human mind. In Revelation, Jesus minces no words with those who pursued salvation by works, calling them a "synagogue of Satan" (Rev. 2:9). And Satan is definitely in on the game. A man we worked with who heard demonic voices would frequently hear messages encouraging him toward good works. One of the main messages the voices told him was that he had to read more and more and more of his Bible. If he did not read more, he felt condemned. It was the same for other religious duties. The demon would praise him for any religious work, but if he tried to abide in God's love, the demon would fight.

I spent two years of my own life trapped in such a pit of legalism and works that I lived in sheer terror of doing something horrible and being raptured to hell. I had come to believe that only a Christian who lived completely free of sin could be accepted by God, so I worked harder to not sin. But the sin got worse and I became more terrified. The more terrified I became, the more I sinned. I had massive lists of Scriptures that I interpreted in the most fearful possible way because I was in such fear. Every judgment passage of the Bible seemed to scream directly at me. I felt completely alone in this war of conscience. If this is you, take comfort, you're in good company – the Reformation itself was started by a monk named Martin Luther when he confronted and found the way out of this exact problem.

The torture finally ended when I decided I would simply pretend God loved me and had forgiven me even though I wasn't really sure. As soon as I began to imagine the perfect love of

God coming to me without any conditions, the illusion melted. I realized it wasn't imaginary at all: God really had forgiven me and loved me completely apart from anything I could do. I stepped into the river of His love and have never gone back.

Before then, I even used to let Satan cut me off from God if I went 56 in a 55 mile/hr speed zone. This is what Jesus lambasted the Pharisees for – straining out a gnat while swallowing a camel. Eventually, I decided to trust God over the gnats and start straining out those camels. I don't let the devil cut me off on the highway of God any more. I read my Bible when I want to, and do not feel condemned when I don't. I worship because I love the presence of God. I pray because I want to encounter God in my heart. The only effort involved is deciding to stop what I am doing and receive from God.

Satan's trap is always to put a reason in front of us why you can't receive God's love. Something you have or haven't done. If you manage to address that reason, a new reason will arise. The list will never end. These are accusations against you designed to keep you in works. As long as you believe there is some reason why you are not "good enough," you are in works. Christ put the endless reasons to death on the Cross.

Another favorite trick of the devil is to pressure us with extreme urgency about being perfectly free from sin now. This seems Christian – God wants us free immediately, right? What happens though, when you believe you must be perfectly free from all sin immediately, is you become fearful. You start trying to do all kinds of things to fix yourself, and you're back into works. If Christianity is about being instantly perfect, then not only is no-one you have ever met actually saved, but it's no longer Good News -- it's an impossible yoke. "Be ye perfect now or else," is not the voice of God—it's the voice of the devil.

Many holiness-oriented preachers unwittingly feed this problem. They preach hard against sin, but fail to offer its real solution. They are preaching a half gospel – they lead you to the Cross but never tell you what to do when you get there. This means that those living in rebellion who need the conviction piece of the gospel will be convicted, but those already wanting to live right with God will become anxious and start trying to eliminate sin through human effort. A holy life is not the result of anxiety about your salvation. If it were, Paul could never have instructed us to "be anxious for nothing" (Phil 4:6). Anxiety about your salvation produces outward holiness, inward sin, and a lot of work to cover it up. A truly holy life comes from perfect security in your salvation. That perfect security comes to you not because you're free from sin already, but because you've turned your heart and life away from sin and toward God.

Are you secure in your salvation? If you are all worked up about it because you have not been able to get sin out of your life, you are living the Christian life backwards. Your sincere desire to be free from sin is the sign that you are a Christian and is enough to be secure in Christ. People who are not really saved do not have this concern. They are always looking for loopholes so they can sin more. You do not try to push sin out in order to be secure; you must abide in your security in order to push sin out. Keeping your eyes on your sin is a bottomless pit. Put your eyes on the mercy that the risen Savior has toward you instead.

> Every step you take to please God by human effort is actually a step backwards.

You may not realize your attempts at self-improvement stem from a belief that you are basically good. You cannot improve something that is basically evil. If you could self-improve, you would not need a Savior. Once you come to the place where you realize nothing you could ever do can make up for the fact that you are evil at heart, then you can be changed. Jesus dealt with your sin by giving you a new life in Him. Every step you take to please Him by human effort is actually a step backwards. You access that new life by receiving love, acceptance, and significance from God apart from human effort.

You Must Believe

All of your effort to keep it together leads you back to the same dead end: bringing the offerings of Cain that God will never accept. You must forsake everything you do to be "good" and approved by God in favor of receiving His love toward you. It's not what you do for God; it's what He did for you. When you are done trying to be good, you are ready to enter into the power of God. When you are ready to bring your sinful beliefs into the light of God's love, you are ready to be changed.

God's perfect love and empowering grace are on the other side of your situation, but until you are absolutely certain that not only does He love people in general, but His love applies to you specifically, you can proceed no farther. You will be tossed around by doubts and unable to obtain freedom (Jas. 1:6-7). When it becomes a settled fact that God's love is absolutely toward you—as a sinner—you are on the cusp of breakthrough.

This concept stumps many people because they have conditioned their prayer and worship routines to be about output – what they do for God or say to God. It is so natural to think of prayer as talking to God, and worship as giving to God. But I contend that these ideas are essentially backwards. All prayer and worship begins with receiving what God gives to you.

Jesus says you do not have to babble on like the pagans because God knows your heart, yet this is exactly what many people do. They try to bombard God with their requests so He will hear them. God is not a deaf idol – He knows the thoughts of your heart before you even pray (Mat. 6:7-8). Centuries of religious tradition have led us to interpret the Lord's Prayer as a formula you should either recite to God or as a model of what you should request from God. Yet, a closer look reveals the first half of the prayer is actually receptive. Coming into a deep knowledge of

God as Father is the beginning of all effective prayer. That is His love. Only when you have begun to receive His love in your heart does the rest of the prayer have power and meaning.

You will not be able to break the power of sin or break into deeper realms with God without the ability to receive the grace and love of God. "Thy Kingdom come on earth as it is in heaven" is not simply a thing I say, but it is a mindset which brings the heavenly reality of God into existence on the earth through me. His Kingdom comes to me as I begin to sit in God's presence and allow the reality of His love to completely overtake every thought and emotion of my heart. In this way I become more at one with Him. And as I become one with Him, my thoughts are His thoughts, my prayers are His prayers. I do not simply send up the random thoughts of my mind, I actually express the thoughts of the Holy Spirit back to the Father.

Worship is just the same. I cannot tell you how many worship services I attended feeling dry as a wick. I would stand there and sing, not feeling a thing at all. I was trying to get into it but to no avail. It was not until I changed my posture from one of trying to "give, give, give," in the worship to one of receiving that the worship had transforming power. Now I can find myself lost in the worship as I step up from the weights of this life into the awesome reality of heaven. Great music helps, but my encounter with God does not depend on a certain music style or level of talent on stage. It depends on my connection with God.

This reality is a place which exists in my heart through faith. Because I know what the Word says about God and have chosen to believe in it, there is a place in my heart to visit. I do not see God, I do not see angels or anything else interesting, but I experience what it is like to be close to God. I disbelieve in any and every barrier that could be between us. I allow His love to flow through to me.

FAITH OR FEAR

All faith is rooted in the absolute certainty of God's love for you. Fear is when you disbelieve it. If faith is the state of mind which brings God's will to pass on the earth, then fear is the state which brings about Satan's will in your life. When your life is full of fear, it is always based on "what if" scenarios. Because you live in a fallen world, where people do evil and can die, there is no rational end to these scenarios. They begin with the reasonable and escalate to the absurd. What if you get hit by a car? What if your plane crashes? What if a man leaps from the bushes while you are taking your walk? What if you run out of gas even though your tank is full? You may try to address these fears by taking more and more precautions, but they always create a smaller and smaller prison cell. Fear is the pit with no bottom.

The terror of your salvation is the most fundamental kind of fear. Until you are perfectly secure in it, Satan can control you through the fear of death (Heb. 2:15). You must drive out this fear by the perfect love of God (1 John 4:18). As you allow God's securing love to penetrate deep into your heart, the fear melts away. Until you let love win out, your faith is unstable. You may feel good sometimes and in terror the rest of the time. Once you are secure in your salvation, death is nothing but a first class ticket to heaven. This takes the bottom out of the bottomless pit. This kind of thinking allows you to take your faith right to the edge because Satan has no power over the one who has no fear.

Coming into the perfect love of God also means letting go of the "what if" scenarios. In Psalm 91 we read about the awesome security that God promises us in life. Every kind of fear you could possibly have is covered there: sickness, death, and harm, by day or by night, you can place your perfect trust in God. This is the kind of faith Jesus walked in every day of His life. He was utterly fearless because He was perfectly secure in God. He could walk through a murderous crowd because He knew God would protect him in the midst of a fallen world. He could sleep in a deadly storm because He was a new creation, not subject to the frailties of the old. This is an awesome place of security.

When the three Hebrew prophets in the book of Daniel refused to bow down to worship the golden image, they boldly declared to the King that God would deliver them—but even if He did not, they would never bow down and serve him (Dan. 3:17-18). In other words, they had great confidence in God to deliver them, but even if the worst case came true, they would still never be controlled by fear. You can have faith every day of your life that God will protect you, but even if you die, Satan still can't have you because you know your eternity is with God. Fear need never be in control again.

UNBELIEF

Nothing can be proven beyond all possibility of doubt. I met a man in college who told me if he ever witnessed a miracle he would sooner believe his entire life was a hallucination than believe in God. When the audible voice of God spoke to Jesus, you would think it would have been unmistakable, yet John says that "some said it thundered" (John 12:29). Their level of disbelief was so great that they were deaf even to the audible voice of God! The same thing happened in Acts 2. Tongues of fire came down from heaven and rested on the disciples. They spoke in languages they did not know, and yet some people actually thought they were just drunk.

Evidence can and does certainly influence your beliefs, but ultimately you make a choice in your heart. How sad it is when I meet people waiting for that experience to convince them that God loves them. I think of the young woman who wants to serve God but is waiting for the feelings of God's love to overwhelm her and convince her that she has not lost her salvation. I think of the man who says he needs those special feelings from God in order to come back to the faith. Or the man who had physically died, had Christ appear to him, and yet came back to life still doubting his salvation!

Such verifying experiences may come, but none are promised. I spent the first 8 years of my Christian life with absolutely no experience of God that I could label as such. I remember being in a powerful meeting where a prophetic minister said "God is here." At the time I was looking around like, "Where is He?" It was only years later that I realized this was the most powerful, life changing meeting I had ever attended. I did not know God enough to know I had encountered Him. I was waiting for a dramatic cloud or something similar to appear, but God is manifest by the love of Christ ruling in your heart. Some people go their whole life without an experience of God's love. God will not force you to let go of your unbelief about His character, and it is that unbelief which is stopping the flow of feelings you may be longing for.

If people can miss the dramatic miracle at Pentecost and the audible voice of God, then clearly what is happening on the outside is not what drives your experience of God. They all physically saw and experienced the same thing. The difference between those who experienced God and those who did not was something on the inside – faith. Your faith is what takes you into the supernatural realm. One group believed in the reality of God, and the other did not. Experiencing any aspect of God, including his love is no different. It is only once you know for sure God loves you far beyond your wildest dreams, and Jesus has dealt with your sin through the Cross, that you will begin to experience His love. No-one can have the certainty for you. And no proof beyond the sacrifice of his Son is promised. You must make the choice to believe.

Experience God

I took a trip to the Grand Canyon with my brother a few years ago. We sneaked out of a conference and drove all the way from Phoenix and back in one afternoon, just to see what it was really like. We were not disappointed. No camera or words can capture how deep the canyon truly is, or how stunning the views are at sunset as you descend from the plateau. It's an experience you remember. It impacts you and stays with you.

This is what needs to happen in the life of every Christian. It's not enough to know that the Grand Canyon of God's love is majestic and beautiful. You have to go and experience it for yourself. Postcards and books simply will not do. Everything I have been telling you so far about God is academic until you actually encounter Him. Christianity is bringing heaven into earth, and the first step is for heaven to be real in you.

For the first few years of my walk with God, this was exactly my problem. I was strongly convicted that Christianity was true, that I was a sinner, that Jesus was my Savior, that the Bible was the Word of God, and that God was like my own dad – a kind and gracious Father. At the end of the day, however, these were things I believed more than things I experienced. My quest to know Him was serious, but it wasn't until I was in a meeting where I saw the speaker minister in the power and love of the Holy Spirit that something clicked inside of me. God's love became real to me—something I could experience and taste.

Now you don't need a powerful meeting to make this happen. God can break into your life at any time through your faith. This section has been about correcting your heart beliefs to allow this to happen. What you need to do now is make it real.

Recall how God is like the sun and your false beliefs are like clouds. You believed He was against you because you didn't feel

Him, but it was all a lie. When you believe in His love, you will begin to feel Him. You believed that some unknown reason was separating you from God's love, but this doubt is itself the reason why you feel separated from Him.

For just a moment, step into imagine a God who loves you so much that He would never let you strike your foot against a stone. Forget for a moment all of the arguments about what He is like or may be like. Bypass that and use your imagination to imagine a God of unbelievably amazing love. Imagine a God who hates every moment you spend in pain and wants you never to have to experience it again. Imagine a God who knows your thoughts and desires, and is with you every moment of your life.

Maybe you have had trouble imagining God is like that. Or maybe you have the same trouble I did – believing His love didn't apply to me. I was always worried about some restitution I had not paid, some unconfessed sin, some ancestral issue… *something* was the next reason why God's perfect peace was not for me. Imagine that none of that matters. Imagine that there is no reason in the world why you cannot bask in God's perfect love. What you are imagining is true. What you have thought before is the imagination. You may have to fight to exchange the two, but it is worth it.

John G. Lake once said, "Hell is distraction." The more I work with those in deep bondage, the more real this statement becomes to me. Satan does absolutely everything possible to keep you from getting into a place with God where His truth becomes the ultimate reality. Have you noticed when you sit down to pray, everything you need to do next week suddenly comes to mind? These are the distractions designed to keep you out of the place of encountering God. When you get into the place of God's presence, nothing else matters. There will be time for earthly concerns later, but now is the time to experience heaven.

Recently, we worked with someone who was constantly bombarded by voices. We knew he could break through to the peace of God anyway, but we needed an example to show him. So we did a little demonstration. I asked my ministry partner to begin to commune with God while I made all kinds of distracting movements and noises. My partner did not flinch because he had learned to tune into God, rather than the distractions of this world. Focus is a choice. You choose what to tune into and what to tune out. You can come to the place where literally nothing else matters. Nothing can be more important than allowing God's love to penetrate the deepest places in your heart. The man with the voices then began to focus on God's love and shut the voices out. In just a few minutes, he began to experience a place in God that Satan could not touch – the place of absolute focus on God.

I am reminded of another young man I was ministering to years ago. He was a very bright individual who had been converted from an Eastern religion. His mind was always racing and it was hard to even have a conversation with him because he was so anxious. One night, during a time of extended ministry, we began to pray for him and told him to clear every thought except Jesus. We asked him to focus on God's perfect love toward him. Initially he said, "I can't, I can't! There are too many other things in my head!" But we encouraged him to put those things aside and just allow the love of God to come through. After a few minutes, he finally broke through. You could see it all over him. For the first time since we had met, he seemed relaxed both physically and emotionally. In fact, the touch of God was so deep that they had to carry him out of the meeting. The Spirit of God flooded his soul when he put everything else aside and broke into the love of God.

As I sit in God's presence, I imagine the place of perfect heavenly intimacy with Him, where all things are possible, and I literally force everything else out of my mind. I remove every thought and concern of this world. I remove every contrary thought. I simply do not entertain them. The Word of God and His truth become the only reality. I bring everything that can separate me from the perfect Christ life into the light of His love and move deeper. As I move into this place, the doubts become silent. God becomes my reality.

What is stopping you from breaking into the love of God? Is it distraction, false belief, or something else? Whatever it is, make the decision right now that you will never let it come between you and God again. The Father sent His Son to die so He would be the only thing that would ever be between you and Him.

This experience and reality is what you need to live a successful life with God. Do not give up until you have broken through everything and anything that could keep you from the Father's love. If you are stuck, I encourage you to work with a pastor or mentor who experiences God more than you do, in order to help you get the breakthrough. When God's love is the most real thing in your life, then you experience true Christianity. Christianity can't work for you without it. Even repentance cannot stick without it. Experiencing God and His love is the fuel in the fire of your life with God.

~ Part IV ~

Repent

What is Repentance?

If you have not come to that place of accepting full responsibility for your problems yet, you need to return to the beginning of this book and process it some more. Nothing is going to help you until you are ready to take responsibility and turn to God. I say this again because the failure to accept responsibility is the primary problem for most people in contemporary culture—*especially* those with the biggest problems. You need a deep acceptance of this before anything in this section can help you.

If you have come to the place where you accept responsibility, have surrendered your life and desires, and have accepted God's love as a fact in your life, then you are ready to really change. This change is called repentance. Your conviction of God's love toward you, and His reconciliation with you, is what gives God's promises real power. Building upon your knowledge and experience of God's love, you can drive sin out of your life.

Although repentance is one of the main themes of the New Testament, there is a lot of confusion surrounding it. Most people think repentance is feeling sorry for something you do. When you sin and hurt someone else, you feel bad and say you're sorry. Feeling sorry and apologizing is not repentance. Neither is trying not to do it anymore. Your behavior may make the other person feel better, but it does not actually change anything at the deepest levels. After bad feelings have worn off, most people go right back to what they were doing because you never broke the underlying root.

TAKE ACTION

Repentance requires you to take action. This is hard for many Christians to realize because they have defined grace to mean, "God does everything and therefore I can do nothing."

This false definition of grace is a smokescreen which keeps you from having to take action and therefore keeps you in bondage. It is exactly what the devil wants you to think. He wants you to think you have no ability or power to influence your situation.

The idea that you cannot do anything to change your situation is a centerpiece of most demonic religions and philosophies. They teach that you cannot influence your future. They say if you were born a slave because that was your fate, or you became great because it was your fate. The course is mapped out and predetermined for you. Perhaps if you are lucky you can do something to improve a future life, but for now you have to accept where you are.

Thank God Jesus came and demolished this fatalism. Jesus did not come saying you should accept your problems and future. He came and offered you a path to freedom. He put the power back in your hands, and this is exactly what Satan does not want you to see. It is God's love and grace which enables you to make and maintain the choice to believe in Him (John 6:44; 10:29). But ultimately it is still you who must make the choice. It is God's power that is at work in your salvation, but it does not happen all by itself. God gives the power, but you have to make it work.

When you first get saved, many people experience a time of joy where their feelings are aligned with God and everything seems easy. Eventually this wears off. At this point, some people simply stop and wonder where God went. This is the wrong response. You had those feelings because you believed God. Are you are wait on feelings? When your feelings are against the choice they you are trying to make, do you give up? If you were waiting around for a feeling or experience in order to get saved, you might still be waiting. Salvation is not in feelings. It is in your decision to believe and base your life on truth.

In the same way, you Christian walk is not a passing feeling, it is a lifetime commitment to follow God. Many people have powerful experiences and still walk away. Bob Dylan did. He had a power encounter with God, cut a few Christian albums, and then returned to his old ways. On the other hand, some people have no experience at all and yet live long, productive

Christian lives. It comes down to the decision. Experience or not, you make a decision in response to the truth.

If I gave you ten million dollars right now to renounce Christ, would you do it? What if I put a gun to your head, would you do it? Every Christian I've ever asked says no to these questions. Why would you say no? It is because you have made a decision deep in your heart that no matter what, you will not turn away from God.

Now, could you actually renounce Christ if you wanted to? Yes, but you have already decided that come what may, you will not do it. Your faith in Christ is a choice you made to believe what God said over what anyone else says. Salvation happens because God did something and you chose to believe and act on it. Not only did you make an initial choice, but you made a resolution, a permanent choice, that you will not even entertain another option. When you make this kind of a decision, everything in the world will come against you. Friends and even family may reject you, but you do not back down because you know Jesus is salvation. Even if the going gets tough, you do not back down because you know it is right and you are going to stand on what you believe no matter what. You push out even the possibility of another option.

This is the same kind of decision which breaks the power of sin in your life. Until you decide to fight for freedom and what is right, no matter what the opposition, you will be stuck. You are not powerless in this situation because you can decide to believe God and act accordingly. There is no magic substitute for you taking action. There are things you can do to help make the right kind of decision and reinforce it, but ultimately it all begins with you saying, "I know this is the right thing and I am going to do it no matter what." All too often people say things like, "I don't know how," or "I don't know what to do," when they really mean they are just not willing to fight for it.

BECOME SINGLE MINDED

Most people trying to get free from sin have some truth. The problem is, they also have a lot of error. You can go from one ministry to another and get a little information here, and a little bit there, and become an expert at talking about your problem. You can know more about your sin and ways to fix it than anyone else alive. This expertise does not produce freedom, however, because knowing about something is not the same as taking action on it. You must apply God's solution at the level where nothing can shake it.

This problem was demonstrated to me vividly when one man we were ministering to told us, "I think I should pray, but the devil doesn't agree, so what should I believe?" Of course the devil doesn't agree — that's the point! There should not be any need to check and see if the devil will permit you to believe the truth. I can tell you in advance that he will pressure and distract you until either you back down *or* he finds out you will never back down. In order to get free, you need to stand on the truth, turn from error, and not back down. Do not let the devil or anyone else intimidate you.

Until you make the same kind of rock-solid decision to move against the sin you are struggling with as you did when you got saved, you will stay a slave because you are double-minded (Jas. 1:8). A double-minded person never stands on the truth long enough for it to work. You try one quick fix and when it does not produce immediate results, you switch to the next quick fix. When you feel overwhelmed by sin, you roll over and feel defeated. This kind of mindset will never produce results. You need to become absolutely certain of the truth and absolutely resolved to walk it out if you want to get free. Your decision against sin is a decision to win a war. You may have ups and downs, but when the going gets tough, you will not give up. You will only become more serious. You must decide to believe God regardless of anything you feel, and keep on believing until you are free.

You must come to the point where you are *not even open* to feelings that would sway you. You may feel discouraged, hopeless, or tempted to the utmost. You may even be tempted to quit believing you can get free and want to give up. A real decision which produces victory is one that says no amount of opposition or feelings are going to sway you. Are you open to feelings which would cause you to doubt Christ and His Word? No. You make a decision to stop entertaining these kinds of thoughts and feelings, and you will not have them any more. Real faith begins when you have a resolution in your heart just like you do for salvation – "I am going to get free or I will die trying."

Ultimately, repentance comes down to this simple decision. Sin, however, makes it seem complex. That is why the rest of this book is dedicated to helping you understand the anatomy of sin and methods for confronting it. The explanations and techniques I will present in the next sections are like training wheels to help you develop the heart discipline of repentance. When you are doing it right, repentance is simple—not a long, complex process. Repentance is not a formula. Formulas are for people who do not want to repent. Repentance is changing your heart and taking action.

WHEN DO YOU REPENT?

It is natural to think of repentance as a long laundry list of things they did in the past. Many deliverance processes are built around this concept. You dig into what you did, or what happened to you, and repent of that. Some ministers even teach that you should repent for something someone else did long ago in your family line. Although you certainly can carry significant baggage from the past, and dealing with it can affect real change, this is not repentance either. First of all, you cannot repent for something someone else did—not any more than you can get saved for someone else. Repentance is about you! And it is about now. You cannot change the past. The only reason the past even matters is if it affects you or others in the present.

On the flip side, some people associate repentance with promises of what they will not do in the future. You make promises to yourself and others that you will not do the same bad thing again. You make resolutions and put systems in place to stop yourself. You may even give yourself a super-spiritual pep talk, complete with extended prayer, Bible time, and spiritual exercises to motivate you. While these are great activities to help you feel better and get refocused on God, they do not constitute repentance either. In fact, sometimes they are just ways to medicate the pain stemming from your need to change.

> **God's focus is not on what you did, but on who you are.**

So what is repentance really? It is changing who you are, now. Although repentance includes freeing you from the past and redirecting your future, the focus of real repentance is on changing the present. God's focus is not what you did, but who you are. Repentance is getting rid of your present desire for sin. Mere resolutions and spiritual activity fail because your heart desires must change. Repentance is addressing those desires. Repentance is changing beliefs which lead to sinful behaviors. You know you have really repented when you do not desire to start down the path which took you there again.

It is liberating to know that repentance is now. It means you do not have to dredge up ancient history to get right with God. It means you do not have to make promises you can't keep. And most importantly it means you can have freedom *right now*. You do not have to wait for a thunderbolt to strike or a special grace. The Holy Spirit is ready at any moment to cleanse you of sin.

THE LIFE OF FAITH

You were born a sinner. When you got saved the nature of Jesus came into you. This means that the full nature of God is available to you in seed form. It does not mean that suddenly you are no longer a sinner. It means that you now have potential to walk free from sin. There is a lot of confusion about this issue within the Body of Christ. On the one hand, some emphasize sin so much that it seems there is no real possibility of being transformed. On the other hand, some teach the work of Christ on the Cross as if it removes the need to be transformed. These two extremes exclude the obvious answer – you can and should be transformed progressively.

Take look at Romans 8:13, where Paul explains this process: "For if you are living according to the flesh, you must die; but if by the Spirit you are putting to death the deeds of the body, you will live." This verse presents two ways you can live your life. The first option is obvious: live according to the flesh. This simply means do what you are doing. You were born of the flesh, and it takes no effort to continue to be of the flesh. If you do this, you will die.

The second option is Paul's instruction for freedom. Take a careful look. "You are putting" is not something that happened in the past or that you do one time. It is an ongoing process that is active now. This is the Christian life. It is the ongoing process of putting the deeds of the flesh to death. This means that the focus of repentance, confession, and anything you do to move away from sin is not in the past, it is in the present. It is not something you did once, but something you continually do. Being born of the Spirit and given the nature of God was a one-time event, but you living by the new nature instead of the old is a continuous process.

Romans 8:13 teaches that who you are naturally is death, but who you are in Christ is eternal life. This means that repentance is not about a repair job on your natural person. Repenting is about moving away from your natural thoughts and abilities and into the supernatural thoughts of God. This is important to understand. I am going to teach you some exercises in this section of the book to help you to get to the root of your beliefs and turn toward God, but it is important for you to understand that repentance is about turning to God, not just digging into sin. An unbeliever can change a belief or habit, but your goal is God's identity and personality operating through you. Your goal is to get into the place of being one with God through the Spirit.

Identifying heart beliefs is simply a way of moving out of unbelief and into faith, moving out of who you naturally are and into your supernatural identity as a child of God. These beliefs are like "hooks" that keep you in the natural world. In the next section, I'm going to teach you how to identify and expose these heart beliefs, but you need to understand that the point of exposing them is to turn away from them and toward God. The point is not to dig and dig until you know all of the roots of all of your sins. This kind of examination has no end. You will become inward focused instead of God focused, and you'll get depressed from staring at your natural man. The reason "why" you sin is because you are a sinner, born of the flesh and inclined toward sin. Instead, gaze into the face of God, and cooperate with him to unhook you from the false beliefs that have tied you to the earth through sin.

This is what it means to "live by faith." It is the continuous process of turning away from your natural desires, natural feelings, and desire for sin, and standing in your supernatural identity as a child of God. It is not simply turning away from sin, it is turning to God. When you turn away from your earthy life and to God, you are repenting. When you move from passivity to action, you are repenting. When you move from lies to truth, you are repenting. When you move from your boring life into fellowship with God, you are repenting.

How Sin Works

You cannot simply grit your teeth against your sin. You may be reading this book because you've already tried this and failed. Repentance is about making the kind of decision which will allow you to receive the grace of God to overcome your sin. Making decisions is always important, but you need to make the right kind of decision for it to be empowered by God. Millions of people make New Years Resolutions every year only to give up a few days later. This is because the resolution they are making is like resolving to stop coughing when you have a cold. You can try and try, but you have to remove the actual cold. In the same way, you cannot change what you are doing until you deal with its fundamental cause.

Think of your behavior like a plant. The leaves and fruit of a plant are fed through the stem and branches. As long as the plant is alive, it will produce them. The stem of the plant is fed through the roots. As long as there is a root, the plant still has life. This is why, for example, grass becomes brown in the winter. Above the ground it appears dead, but below the surface it is still alive.

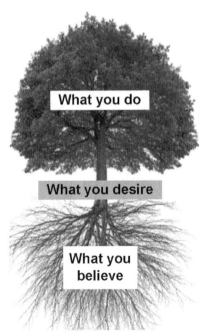

Many people make strong resolutions to stop producing the fruit of sin, but it does not work. In fact, it is a deception which causes you to think you have repented when you have not. If you try to change your behavior without changing your desires, you will be in works and legalism. Although a change in behavior is essential, a change of heart must be at the root of any change in behavior.

Repentance is not simply an action plan or a regimen of discipline. If you have only made a resolution to stop, you will go back to your sin as soon as you get tired of the discipline. You cannot fight back the nature of the plant until you cut it at the root. Trying to change your behavior by making resolutions about what you will or will not do is like trying to get an apple tree to stop producing apples. You can't do it. It's in the DNA. What is needed is change at a more fundamental level.

Let's take a simple example: cigarettes. When we were running our recovery program, most of the guys came with some level of nicotine habit. The difference between those who truly repented and those who did not was obvious. You can be off cigarettes for a year and still not have repented if you still are longing for one. We tried a policy of gradual reduction to help one man kick his habit, but the fewer cigarettes he got, the more he cherished and savored them. It wouldn't have mattered if we had gotten him down to 0. He had not repented. He still wanted his habit. He would have simply been what some people call a "dry drunk."

Whatever you desire, you will become consumed with having. You may be able to grit your teeth against it for awhile, but you will either live a life of misery or eventually give in to what you desire. If you keep longing for sin but still manage to tough it out while not doing it, not only will you be miserable, but the sin will still be in your heart. This is why Jesus called the Pharisees "whitewashed tombs." They were dealing with the outside without dealing with the inside (Matt. 23:25-28). The Pharisees had mastered keeping up appearances: not sinning by the letter of the law but also not having any heart change. Just like putting a cork on a fizzing bottle, the more you try to hold sin in, the more pressure builds up. Trying to stop sin from the outside will actually make the sin worse.

Therefore, to break the power of sin, you have to break the desire. Until you do, you will find sin creeping out at every point. This is because your behavior stems from your desires.

YES, YOU DO WANT IT

Maybe you are thinking to yourself, "Ok, but I don't want my sin. It's ruining my life." Yet you keep returning to it, feeling helpless. How does this happen? A closer look reveals that what you really do not want are the consequences. Consequences are usually what drive you to seek help. You don't want your wife to throw you out of the house so you go to AA. You don't want to go to back to jail so you see the probation officer. You stop looking at porn because you don't want to lose your ministry. Consequences cause you to make changes, but if you still want to drink, do drugs, or look at pornography, your underlying desires haven't changed.

Some people realize they are only changing in response to consequences, but many do not. They think because they really want to get cleaned up that they have in fact repented. This is a deception. As soon as the negative consequences go away, they start right back down the same road they were on. And if they could have the sin without any negative consequences, they would never seek help. Consequences motivate you to want a change and that's good, but the change you need is to stop loving the sin, consequences or not.

> You think that because you want to get cleaned up, that you have repented, but it's a deception.

Maybe you have moved beyond wanting freedom just because of consequences and realize that what you are doing is really wrong in God's eyes. You say to yourself, "I know this is wrong—I want to stop." You have a sincere desire to do what is right before God regardless of the consequences, but you still cannot seem to break the power of sin. Why not? It is because knowing something is wrong and no longer wanting it are two different things. Everyone knows cheating on your spouse is wrong, yet many people do it anyway. You may feel horrible guilt, cry, and promise you will never do it again, only to find yourself back in the same place. You are entirely sincere in knowing God hates adultery, and want to obey God, but you are not able to. What is going on?

You are struggling because there is a conflict between your desire for sin and your desire to be right with God. You are what James calls "double-minded." It is stunning to realize, but knowing and even agreeing with God that something is wrong will not stop you. I spent years mired in sin because of this deception. I sincerely wanted to be right with God. I sincerely wanted to do what He wanted me to do, but I could not do it. I could not stop because at a deeper level I found sin desirable. I, like many people, would have said I was "struggling with sin." What I didn't realize was that I was struggling because of the conflict between my desire to be right with God and my desire for the pleasure of sin. I was double-minded.

A lot of what we call "struggling with sin" is actually double -mindedness. I'm not talking about the struggle of opposition you feel when you are on the right path with God. What I'm talking about is the struggle of going back and forth, experiencing victory and then defeat and inner turmoil. This struggle comes from double-mindedness. The struggle is you wavering between which way you will go. You have not decided at a deep level to stop desiring the sin. You are holding on to something while at the same time knowing it is wrong. You feel pulled back and forth by the grip of sin because it is lodged deep in your heart and you do not want to let it go. Any time you have this kind of struggle, it is revealing an area where you still want sin. The struggle will end when you release every hold and desire for sin in your heart.

This does not just apply to exciting sins. It applies to anything you can struggle with: anger, rejection, unforgiveness, depression, anxiety, fear, etc. These things may not feel desirable but they offer you something you want. Anxiety, for example, offers you a false sense of security. You believe by thinking about it over and over again you will feel secure, but you actually feel less secure. What about anger? Although we think of anger as a negative emotion, it can make you feel good sometimes. When you release your negative emotions – at someone else's expense – this makes you feel better. Or take depression. Although misery will go on longer if you are depressed, it gives a strange sense of comfort and safety. Until you decide you do not want those feelings, anxiety, depression, and anger will stay with you. The promises these sins offer you are false, but you embrace them anyway. You'd rather have the pain of feeling bad than the pain of getting free.

Escaping from sin means escaping from the deception that you do not desire it. You do. Feeling horrible afterwards is not real change. Knowing there are consequences is not enough. Knowing God says it is wrong is not enough. It is not real change. Although you may not want the consequences, if the sin is there, at some level you desire it. Seeing this reality puts the power back in your hands.

WHAT YOU BELIEVE

The root of the matter ultimately goes back to what you believe about the sin. If I offered you a cup of mud, would you drink it? No, of course not. Why not? Because you do not believe it is desirable, something you would want. What if I offered you your favorite candy bar? You would take it because you think it is something to be desired. Sin is the same way. Whatever you believe about sin will determine your desire for it. The kind of decision you need, therefore, is not a resolution about your behavior but a deeper change in your beliefs. You have to change what you believe about the sin. You have to bring your thoughts and emotions in line with the truth of what God says about it. When you do this, it will not seem desirable anymore and it will have no power over you. You cannot crave something you hate.

As long as you think your sin is desirable or pleasurable, you are in a state of unbelief. God certainly does not think your sin is desirable. In order to break out, you must disbelieve in sin and believe in God. This is repenting. You have repented when you believe God at the level that you stop wanting it. You come to the place where you would stop even if there were no consequences. Believing sin is undesirable may sound straightforward, but it is much more than saying to yourself, "This is not desirable." The change of belief you need is total. It must affect everything you think and feel. Simple confessions do not accomplish this. They only put a coat of white paint over the substructure of sin.

Getting really free of sin requires you to drive out even the possibility of being tempted. We have been told it is impossible not to be tempted since even Jesus was tempted, yet this skews the facts. Jesus was only tempted on two occasions in His life that we know of. First, He was tempted in the wilderness, and second in the Garden of Gethsemene. We have no indication He experienced any of the extended and deep wrestling that we call temptation. He defeated temptation in the desert and simply walked above it until He reached the point of going to the Cross.

Temptation is not the result of a demonic attack that you must be a victim of, or a state of nature which you cannot overcome. In Christ, you can drive it out. The Bible teaches that temptation occurs when your sinful desires pull you away (Jas. 1:13-15). What you are thinking about when you are tempted is the temporary emotional pleasure you would experience from feeding your flesh. Look closer – thinking about the sin is itself a sin. As you meditate on and consider it, you are relishing the feelings it gives you. You are committing the sin in a virtual world. Such fantasies are actually ways of tasting the pleasure of the sin, which makes you hungry for more until finally you act on it. You must close yourself down from even tasting the pleasure of thinking about the sin. In order to do this, you must change what you believe.

EMOTIONS

When Eve took the fruit in the Garden of Eden, the Scripture says she "saw that it was good for food and delightful to look at, and that it was desirable for obtaining wisdom." Based on information from her flesh and the lie of Satan, she made a false judgment. She thought the fruit which was going to kill her was good! She disbelieved God because of an emotional experience. How do you respond when your emotions lie to you? Do you simply believe them? Are you waiting for God to magically change them?

The emotional pleasure you experience when you sin is what convinces you sin is desirable—something you really want. In essence, you believe your emotions instead of God. Once you participate in the sin, your belief in it gets reinforced by the high that comes from it: 'I get drunk. I feel nice. I believe drinking works. It is something I want." But saying you want to drink is another way of saying, like Eve, that your sin is "good." That's where her sin began and that's where ours does too. When you commit the sin, it corrupts you further (Rom. 1:21-32). The more you sin to meet your inner need, the more you want it. Even though it is ruining your life, you still think it is good because of the emotional pleasure it gives you. Your flesh becomes wired to crave something unhealthy to meet your needs but because unhealthy things never satisfy; they always create a deeper craving for more.

Think of your beliefs as having two components – what you think and what you feel. When God's grace is operating in your life, your feelings and your thoughts change. Your thoughts and emotions work in a cycle. What you feel leads to what you think, and what you think influences your feelings. You see something you want, feel the grip of desire and then think, "That is good. I want that." In turn, you think something is good and so when you see it, you have excited emotions about it. The problem is that your flesh in its natural state craves and generates emotions for things which are not good. Therefore you develop a strong cycle of thoughts and emotions locking you into sin, and the more you feed the cycle the stronger it gets. In order to arrest this cycle, you must repent and disbelieve the thoughts and feelings which are contrary to what God says – they are lies.

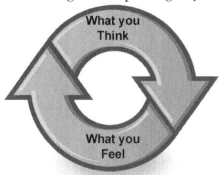

In our relativistic generation, many people think that if you feel it, it must be true. But you can see from Eve's experience that this is simply not the case. Her feelings lied to her. When she believed them she started the cycle of death. Your feelings are not the truth, they are an indicator of what you believe. Until she believed Satan's word about the tree, she did not see it as beautiful. She probably saw it as deadly and something to avoid. Your feelings tell you what *you* believe, not whether the belief is actually true. For this reason, you cannot follow your feelings or you will simply be a slave to any impulse of the flesh. Breaking the pattern of sin means becoming rewired not just in how you think, but in how you feel as well. The emptiness and craving you feel which push you toward sin must be driven out.

Some people have sought to deal with this problem by simply shutting down their emotions. This is like shutting down the instruments when flying an airplane. The instruments are telling you that something is wrong and you need to either make a course correction or fix the instruments themselves. You cannot ignore your emotions any more than you can ignore the instruments in the cockpit. Ignoring emotions will not make sinful desires go away. In order to remove the desire, you must remove the beliefs which support it, then close yourself to those feelings and open your heart to the love of God.

Suppressing your emotions does not get rid of them. They will simply lurk underneath the surface. On the surface, the sea is calm, but below, it is a jagged reef. Emotions must be surfaced and confronted in order to have true peace. Your emotions and beliefs often lie hidden beneath the surface of your personality until the moment of opportunity. You may not feel any emotion or think any thought toward sin until the moment it is presented to you, at which point the thoughts and feelings will manifest. They were there all along, just suppressed. In order to break free, you need to bring them all to the surface and remove them completely. You cannot simply confess or pretend you do not have them. You need to bring them out onto the field of battle and defeat them.

Bring It to God

Hopefully you learned from the first half of the book that God cannot heal what you do not reveal. If you do not accept responsibility for your sin then God's power will not work. Furthermore, if you do not open your heart to allow God to deal with it, God's love will not apply. This chapter is about making this a reality for you.

We worked with a man recently from another country who had a very rough upbringing in a culture where strength is valued more than mercy. At school he felt abandoned, inside his house he faced a domineering mother, and outside his house he faced thugs. This led him to be quite depressed. He was a difficult case for his pastor. The pastor was a very spiritual person who had cast the demon out of this man multiple times. The man himself was quite proactive and ready to apply any spiritual counsel given to him, but nothing had really worked. He would experience temporary relief but soon go back to his state of deep depression.

After talking with him for a while, it soon became obvious what was blocking him from freedom. Instead of bringing his problems to God to heal them, he was trying to fix them himself. That's what the macho culture where he was from told him he should do. And that attitude was reflected in his Christian life. To get him free, we had to teach him to reverse this process. Instead of trying to fix himself for God, he needed to bring problems out into God's presence. As he went through several layers of this, he experienced a miraculous turnaround and a renewal in his walk with God.

In order to bring your problems to God, it helps a lot to be able to experience God in the first place. This is what the last part of the book was about – helping you to have a love encounter with God which you can build upon to experience true victory. It is only from the place of God's love that you will be able to experience His healing. For most people, worship music can help create the right atmosphere for this to happen. Once you know how to have a love encounter with God, you will be able to bring things you have been hiding into His presence. So the first step is to get into God's presence the best way you can.

Then you must expose the things which you have been hiding from God. This may be quite foreign to you. Whenever sin gets close to the surface, the natural human response is to bury it or push it aside. This is even truer when you think God can see it. Just like Adam and Eve, we invent coverings for ourselves by pushing sin undercover into darkness. The path to freedom is doing just the opposite: bringing the sin into the light of God's presence. Not in a brash way, but in a way that says, "Lord, this is real. I want you to know I admit to it, and I want you to change me." When you get comfortable with the fact that your sin is there and God knows it, and still He loves you, you can begin to allow Him to remove it.

Now you may have buried a lot of pain in places you do not want to deal with. Or you may be addicted to looking good and being perfect for everyone, including God. If this is where you are, then you are not coming to God through the Cross. You are coming through your own works, and it's no wonder that Christianity hasn't worked for you.

Or you may have been taught that since you have already been made righteous, there is nothing to bring to God. This is a false conclusion. You have been made righteous in the sense that you are saved and going to heaven. You are righteous in the sense that God's Kingdom is operating in your life in seed form. But the Kingdom of God is like a garden plant (Matt 13:32). You grow it and nurture it until it takes over your life. When you have sin, you acknowledge and confess it. There is a place for declaring your righteousness in Christ, but it is after you get real with your sin. In order to be free, you must bring your sin into God's presence, admit that it is real, admit that it is you, and then let God take it from you. Next, I will present a series of practical exercises to help you do just that.

In the last chapter, I discussed the anatomy of sin in your heart, how it sets up through your beliefs, emotions, and identity even when you do not know they are there. The craving for sin happens at a primal level which you may have never explored before. You do not always need to understand the sin process or your particular false beliefs to get free, but it can be quite helpful if you do. It is much easier to defeat something you can identify. What are the thoughts and feelings which are driving you to sin?

The simplest way to surface your beliefs is to visit the moment of temptation in your imagination. In your mind's eye, go to the point where you sinned or were tempted to sin. What were the thoughts and feelings you were experiencing? Can you put words to them? Now imagine yourself in the same situation choosing to do the right thing. You will feel a pull back to the sin. What is the pull? What are the thoughts and feelings associated? This is where the grip of sin is.

Another way to expose your hidden beliefs is what we call the "heart ping." You bounce truth off of your heart to see what comes back. Start with a Scripture relevant to your situation. For example if you feel disconnected with God, you could quote, "We were reconciled to God through the death of his Son" (Rom. 5:10). After you speak this truth over yourself, listen to what you think and feel in response. When you say it, do you feel reconciled, or do you feel a hesitation in your heart? If hesitation, what is it? Why don't you feel reconciled? Is there a reason? As you expose these hidden thoughts and feelings, you begin to see what is really inside your heart. These things must be melted away in the presence of God.

These are two techniques that we have found to help you surface false beliefs and feelings not normally in your conscious realm. These are things that you are unintentionally hiding from God. This is in addition to those things that you are more consciously aware of: old hurts, a judgment you have against someone else, or simply the sinful thought and feelings you have all the time but you do not want to bring to God. Regardless of what you have been hiding or how you bring it to the surface, the key thing is that you now bring that which was hidden in darkness into the light and turn away from it.

SOBRIETY EXERCISE

Sometimes a rational look at your sin can be a profoundly sobering experience. This is the thinking component of the cycle. What thoughts do you have which lead you to believe sin is something you want? What if you, for example, were considering cheating on your spouse? You know it is wrong and risky but you cannot control your desires. You are convinced, for sexual or emotional reasons, that the love affair is something you really want. You think it is a candy bar, not a cup of mud. And the more you think about eating that candy bar, the more you want it until eventually you cannot control yourself.

When you step back for a minute and take a rational look at the affair, however, it's a lot less desirable. You will probably never regain the love and trust of your spouse the way you had it before. You may even lose them forever through a divorce. If you have kids and you divorce, your children will experience the consequences for the rest of their lives. They will experience many practical challenges and deep psychological wounds. If you are a man, you will likely have limited visitation rights to your children, and a huge monthly bill you can't afford called "child support." How does that affair look now? Still a candy bar? If you thought more thoroughly about it when that attractive person showed up, you'd begin to have different feelings about it. It would not seem desirable.

This kind of rational analysis is one part of breaking the power of sin in your life. Take a piece of paper and put two columns on it. In the first column, write down everything you like about your sin. In the second column write down everything negative about it. Rarely do the two lists ever compare. The life of freedom is much more desirable. You are deceived in the moment into thinking sin is really desirable. If I said I would give you a million dollars to drink poison would you do it? Of course not. It's not rational. The consequence cancels out any possible benefit. Compare the columns on your list. Decide one by one that none of the poisons you like is worth the death on the other side.

A sober comparison between the costs and benefits of your sin helps to influence your desire but will not work by itself. Plenty of people voluntarily press the self-destruct button on their lives knowing full well what the consequences are. You have to come to a place where you are done needing reasons, explanations, or debate in your mind about sin. First, you settle deep in your heart that what God says about your sin is true. He doesn't just say it is wrong or bad. He says it is undesirable. It is not something you want. When you really believe this, you will stop feeding the desire for sin and become dead to it. It will be like a cup of mud to you. You'll make a decision that no more reasoning is needed. You'll believe what God says and that settles it.

If you think about it, this is the fundamental problem that started the whole process of human sin in the first place. Adam and Eve were given a command. Eve was approached by the serpent who gave her a different idea of truth, so she entered into dialog with the serpent. She had a discussion with the devil about what was right and wrong. As soon as you are having a discussion with the devil about right and wrong, you have already lost. That is because the discussion itself is rooted in unbelief. You stopped believing the truth and now you need to wrestle with whether a lie might be the truth instead. Cut off diplomatic ties with Satan. There is no room for debate with sin.

FALSE BELIEF EXERCISE

The sobriety exercise can help you move toward truth if the sin you are dealing with is something tangible like committing adultery or going to the bar. But often times the sin that needs to be dealt with is more of a belief pattern, such as guilt or worthlessness. In cases like these, it can be helpful to take the belief apart logically.

Let's examine the belief such as, "I am worthless." A belief like this does not stand on its own. It is a summary of thoughts, interpretations of experiences, and emotions. If someone asked you why you believe it, what would you say? What reasons would you give to defend it? What kinds of things are part of a belief like this? Maybe you would point to a series of events like being bullied in school or getting kicked out by your parents. Take a piece of paper and write all the reasons down. Build up the case for your false belief

What is interested about false beliefs is that they are usually built on just a couple of examples, not a comprehensive picture of who you are. People on the outside know you are valuable, but you do not. You have selected a couple negative experiences and drawn a false conclusion, instead of looking at the whole truth. From several events you have made the conclusion that you are worthless, but it is not true.

What you need to do now is refute your own argument. Write down the list of facts which show why your false belief is actually false. Prosecute the case of truth against this lie. Pick it apart. Challenge every piece of evidence you presented for the lie. Ask someone else for help if needed, or maybe even do some study. The goal is to demolish the reasons why you feel like you must believe it. Why is this important?

I worked with a man who hated his home country. He thought it was a terrible place and he never wanted to return. Even thinking about it was a source of pain. Behind this belief was a set of experiences he had in his life before God. They all added up to a negative perception of his country. The problems he identified were real, but the conclusion he reached was not from God. It was not objective reality, but an opinion this man had developed based on his years of pain. And it was more than a single belief. This man's rejection of his own country represented a much larger bondage concerning his life experience as a whole. Underneath his conclusion were painful experiences and false interpretations of numerous events, from being abandoned, to being beaten up, and everything in between.

If he had only confronted the lie that his country was terrible, all the other false beliefs and painful experiences could have remained hidden. In reality his country was simply a representation of deeper issues. They were exposed as we probed it. Building this kind of case can help you expose and confront the deeper issues going on beneath your belief system.

The goal of this exercise is for you to take ownership of believing the truth from top to bottom. You need to reject Satan's interpretation of your life and embrace God's interpretation. In the same way that Satan has a laundry list of accusations and false reasons, God has a laundry list of praises and facts which support the truth you need to believe. I want you to believe the truth not just because God says so, but also because you need to believe and understand all the valuable things about yourself underneath. This is the final step. Reject the lies you wrote down and accept the truth. Turn away from the lies that you have loved and turn instead toward the truth.

When you believe a lie, you are standing in the place of unbelief, where no one can convince you of the truth and everything seems to prove the lie you want to believe. The goal of this exercise was to expose and confront that. Now it is time to move to the place of faith where no set of reasons can convince you into something untrue. You believe what God says is true because He says it is true. Instead of adding more and more reasons to support your old lies, as you stand in faith you will add more facts and experiences to support the truth.

If, at this point, you get stuck with endless questions it is because you are choosing to believe your feelings. You must settle in your heart that you will entertain no more questions. What matters is what God has said. Remember Eve entertained Satan's questions about what God said, and that is where sin began. The Word of God trumps reason and feelings. It is the ultimate truth. You should come to the place where there is no more discussion or rationalization in your heart. God says it is bad, and therefore you will not even entertain the thought of it. Your level of trust for God can become so high that you do not even think about the choice to sin. You recognize the feeling of starting to think about it from far off and can shut it down before it has the smallest foothold. You are closed to the idea of even thinking about it.

HEART CLEANSING EXERCISES

At this point you should have some experience in entering the presence of God and bringing your sin to the surface. The exercises in this next section are designed to help you make these a reality at the heart level of your desires and emotions.

We have developed a "two hand" technique which often helps people get started with this idea. (You may want to do this in worship to make this easier.) Imagine the presence, perfect love, and perfect freedom of God are in one hand. Then in the other hand, imagine the pull of the sin you are struggling with. So now one hand should feel like freedom and the other hand should feel like the pull of sin. One hand contains the truths you learned about God in our "Experiencing God" section. The other hand contains truths you exposed through the surfacing exercises.

Repentance is turning from one hand to the other, turning from the pull of sin to the pull of freedom. Do that now. Feel and weigh the choice in both hands and turn away from sin and toward God. You will likely feel an inner wrestling in the process of turning away from sin and toward God. This means your attachment to the sin has been exposed. Let all of it go and turn to God without looking back. Release everything that could ever draw you to that sin and allow God's love to come in its place. Continue to do this until you feel a complete release from sin.

Another helpful exercise which can bring substance to the repentance process is the "visualization" technique. Go back to your situation of bondage or temptation. Now imagine it differently. Imagine yourself doing the right thing. Turn away from each of the thoughts and feelings drive you down the sinful path, and turn toward the truth of God. There may be pain in your heart that you feel as you imagine the situation. This too has to be released into God's love, which is toward you. Keep doing this until you feel there is nothing left inside you enticing you to sin. Continue this process until you are able to bask freely in the presence of God.

Take it to the next level by visualizing absolute freedom. Imagine your life without ever having this sin again. Imagine what it would be like to be completely free and never turn back. Abide in this reality. Think about it. Imagine the feeling of cleanness and health you will have. Imagine the restored relationships. This is the new reality you can step into. By dwelling here in your heart and removing the obstacles between you and that reality, you are stepping out of the old life of sin and into a new life in Christ where sin has no hold over you.

This visualization technique can be especially helpful when you are dealing with something that is triggered by another situation. For example, when you see your boss you always feel anxiety. Thinking about yourself facing your boss while you are in the comfort of your own home gives you a chance to work through the thoughts and feelings while there is no real danger. Then when the moment comes, you have already developed strength in your heart to stay in the grace of God. The point is that in the moment of pressure, sin can feel nearly impossible to fight. Therefore, confront the problem while you are in control, not when your circumstances have the upper hand.

The same visualization technique can be applied to your dreams. Often when people start down the road to victory, they will notice that suddenly they begin having vivid dreams involving temptation or intimidation. Many feel victimized when this happens. Instead, see this as an opportunity. Instead of worrying about Satan or demonic agencies being at work while you sleep, think of your dream as another way of revealing what is in your heart. You have been winning victories in your conscious realm and now the battle has moved into your subconscious realm. The good news is that you do not have to be a victim even in the dream world. Think of your dream like a manifestation of a spiritual reality. You can step back into it, in your mind's eye, and take dominion. Imagine yourself changing the circumstances of your dream. Fight for control of your heart until you are able to imagine the dream unfolding differently.

Difficult external circumstances function in the same way as dreams. They reveal a deeper level of what is going on in your heart than you normally see. Someone who can remain calm in a coffee shop may be panicked in a storm. The issue of fear and anxiety was always there, but it took a storm to bring it out. Many people are tempted to excuse the situation by saying things like, "But it's normal." Jesus could have easily excused the disciples for their fear in the midst of the storm in the Sea of Galilee—after all, it was a big and dangerous storm. Instead He challenged them to increase their faith. He was in such a place of trust and peace that He was asleep!

I'm not saying that you should condemn yourself if you crack under pressure. Jesus didn't condemn His disciples. I am saying that you should see it as an opportunity to grow in your faith and in the grace of God. The harder the external circumstance, the deeper things in your heart will be exposed, and the stronger degree of faith and conviction you will need to walk in faith.

ICEBERG EXERCISE

Having worked with a lot of people who are addicted to alcohol and drugs, my experience is that there are two kinds of addicts: those who like it, and those who are driven to it by another sin hidden below the surface. For those who simply like to drink and party there is no root beneath what they are doing. The issue that this kind of person must deal with is the love of sin, as we have been discussing. The iceberg exercise is designed to help the other group.

Take, for example the issue of lust. Sex is and can be desirable all on its own, and for many men especially, the problem is basically that simple. However, the issue can be more complex. One of my main problems was what I would call "gender identity." I felt driven to pornography by a sense that being a man was really not that great, which led me to hate myself in a way. This meant that lust, pornography and sexual sins had much more power than if I was simply in it for the fun. As I was healed of these negative self-beliefs, and developed a strong inner sense of confidence and masculinity, the strength of the pull of lust diminished. I had dealt with the sin beneath the sin. The lust was the tip of the iceberg of a more significant understructure of sins. Once I dealt with the powerful

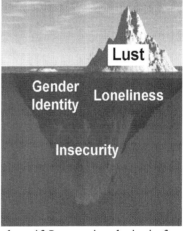

issue underneath, I still had to deal with lust itself, but this would have been impossible without attacking the sin underneath the surface.

My experience is that blackout drinkers and alcoholics often have something bigger beneath the surface too. This is because they drink well past the point where it is fun or even addictive. They drink in a way that is personally destructive. There is something more driving them. And it can be a death spiral. You think you are a worthless person, so you drink. Then you create problems for other people in your life, so you feel more worthless, and you drink more. This iceberg would have alcohol on the top, and under the surface you would have "worthlessness." Even as you fight the urge to drink yourself to death, the more important fight is to destroy the sense of worthlessness that is driving you to the bottle.

For the iceberg exercise, simply draw an iceberg of your own. On the top, put the sin you think you are wrestling with – depression, anxiety, anger, alcohol, whatever it is. Now take a minute and ask yourself if there is more to it than meets the eye. What do you think about when you are about to start your way into sin? What about while you are in the middle of it? What about when you are done? Is there relief? Why? Ask a friend or mentor if they see any pattern. Do you have unresolved issues with your parents or other loved ones? These can give you clues that there is more at work than meets the eye. There can also be more than one root. Put anything from events, to related sins, to thought patterns underneath the surface.

If you found something through this exercise, the key now is to deal with those things as their own problem. For many people with the strongest addictions, I find that it is confronting this giant lurking beneath the surface that is key to freedom. One of the men I worked with could never forgive himself for his sister's death. He thought he had a drinking problem. His drinking problem was minor compared to issues of guilt and self-worth surrounding his sister's death. He had been fighting the drinking for years, but he was fighting the wrong enemy. In fact, he was more comfortable fighting the drinking since it wasn't the real problem. When we got around to addressing the real root problem of his self-worth, he was much more stubborn and difficult. He would not let go of these negative self-beliefs. I explained to him that until he did, he might as well go ahead and drink because there is no way he would be able to stop.

You can now understand why getting to the place of freedom is often a multilayered process. Removing a large sin pattern can involve repenting not just about the issue itself, but often about deeper and more important issue beneath the surface. Before you start attacking sin, it's a good idea to make sure you are attacking the right one. ☺

The techniques presented in this section are simply ways to jump start you on the road to transparency with God and lasting repentance. They are starters to help you grow in the disciplines of the heart. Our team has found that with practice, they become easier and even natural, so that breakthroughs with God get easier with time. Developing these heart disciplines are only one part of the freedom puzzle, however. You will need the teachings in the next chapter if you want to experience the victorious life. The goal is a life of faith, where you are dead to the things of the flesh, and alive to the things of God.

Take Authority

The quickest way to get to hell is to do nothing at all. Since you were born a sinner, and the world is steeped in sin, simply taking no action at all will destroy your life. Taking action is the way out. In the first edition of this book, I put a lot of emphasis on how the heart works because this is the piece which is missing from most other teaching. Receiving God's love and surfacing your sin are not the only components of repentance, however. The other piece is taking action—action that is based on faith. Rise up and take authority over your life, over the devil, and over anything that stops from you experiencing God.

You can see this in the ministry of Jesus, especially His healings. In many of His miracles, Jesus commands the person to take action. This obedient action is the moment of faith. Taking the step of obedience *is* repentance. When Jesus says, "Take up your mat and walk," and you get up, you are moving from a place of passivity and defeat to one of action and victory.

Learning how to deal with heart issues can lead people to try to address sin as if it is an advanced psychological process. The good news is that it is not. The man on the mat did not have to understand his hidden mentality of defeat. He repented of it by standing up and obeying God; the chains of physical bondage fell off of him. Ultimately, that is the same thing you need: a radical desire to obey Jesus at all costs, and a rising up within your spirit to war for your rightful place in God.

CONFESSING THE WORD

If you have been in church long enough, you have most likely been taught to confess the Word. My practical experience is that sometimes confession can be very effective, and other times it doesn't work at all. How can the same thing lead to two different results?

What makes the difference is what is going on inside of you when you do it. The Bible says in Romans 10:9 that if you "confess with your mouth **and** believe in your heart" you will be saved. What you say with your mouth is pointless if you do not believe it in your heart. This is why a lot about confession is backwards. You tell yourself, "I am free in Christ," or "I do not desire to sin," but really you do. The confession intended to help you ends up being a way of covering up instead.

I wish I had understood this when I first started the Christian walk. I kept trying to convince my heart through things that I was saying. I didn't know how to address what was going on at a deeper level. In order to believe rightly, I needed to get real with myself and God about what I really believed first and then bring those things to God to be changed. This is a posture of your heart. Teachers of confession recognize this too, they just use different terms. They often talk about the "heart" and the "mind" not being in agreement.

This is why I have so far emphasized the repentance exercises. You have to get real with God about your false beliefs and work with God to change them. Telling yourself over and over again that do you not or should not believe them will not work. If you do not get honest with God and change your heart, then confessing the Word actually becomes a way of covering up. I have experienced this myself and seen it with a number of people we have helped. People who want to change get frustrated, and people who do not want to change start promoting the doctrine because they can say the words but stay the same.

The kind of confession that does work is one that starts with reality and takes authority it. You get honest with God about where you are, you repent, and then you use confession as an enforcement mechanism. This is the way I have learned to use confession, and I find it very effective.

In order to understand the difference between the two kinds of confession, let's take an example. You can say, "I no longer walk by the flesh," but what do you mean in your heart? Do you mean, "I have not been walking by the flesh, I am not a sinner,

I'm a man of God?" Or do you mean, "God, I have been walking by the flesh and I admit it. Right now I turn away from the flesh and toward your love and power. I am a new creation." Can you see the difference? False confession avoids repentance. True confession enforces repentance. When I declare that, "I no longer walk by the flesh," I am strongly asserting something new in place of something old. I am turning from one to the other. I am repenting.

Confession will help you reinforce and strengthen once you have a change of heart, but until you actually remove the wrong beliefs, it's just part of the cover up. I make strong declarations when I pray as a way of asserting what I really believe, not as a way of trying to convince myself of something I do not believe. I don't try to confess my desire away. I admit it to God, allow Him to deal with it, and then I forcefully declare my new identity.

When I confess, I strongly declare truth over my life and over the lives of those around me. I verbally declare that "Jesus Christ is Lord" and that "Sin can have no power over me." These are ways of rising up and asserting my authority as a believer. They are ways that I step into my supernatural identity as a Christian and out of my identity as a fallen man. This kind of confession produces results because I am starting by admitting reality, turning to God, and asserting His greater reality over it. Confession is you rising up and taking authority over your heart and your life. Just like the man getting up off of the mat, you are responding to God with action based your faith. Confession is not changing things outside of you, rather it is stepping into God so He can change things inside of you. When the inside is changed, the outside will follow.

I challenge you to incorporate this kind of confession or verbally assertive prayer into your lifestyle. Step into your authority as a child of God. This does not have to be complex—what matters is that you are taking control of your emotional and mental life. My wife even will even use the simple confession of "No" or "Yes" in prayer, depending on the situation, as a way of reinforcing truth. Do it forcefully and with confidence. A little mousey declaration is not going to take authority over anything.

These kinds of affirmations powerfully assert who you are and what you intend to be in God.

PRAY IN THE SPIRIT

Authoritative confession is more powerful when used in conjunction with praying in tongues. Regardless of your doctrine, I'm telling you from personal experience that praying in tongues has a powerful effect in the area of repentance and freedom. Some people teach tongues as if there is something almost magical that happens just as a result of you doing it. That is not what I'm talking about here. Tongues is not a magic formula where if you do it enough, amazing things will happen. No doubt that a good routine of praying in the Spirit can bring breakthrough in your life, but when it becomes a formula, it can end up just another way of covering the roots of sin. You feel spiritual, but the grip is still there.

Tongues do, however, give you the ability to break out of an emotional box. Think about it. When you begin to speak in tongues, you are literally short-circuiting the entire emotional-rational process and going straight to God. It is another way of taking authority, stepping out of your identity as a fleshly person, and into your identity as a child of God.

Everyone has felt, at times, like they cannot get into the place in God where they want to be. You feel a desire toward God, but demotivated overall, like you are in a funk or oppressed. The flesh can seem too overwhelming to confront. It is in these times when praying in tongues can break the grip. If I go to God and feel this kind of haze, I stop and go into a mode of praying in tongues mixed with confession to get myself out.

Tongues acts as a trump card to the emotional state you are in. They allow you step back up into the mindset of God regardless of whatever funk you feel like you are in. Speaking in tongues requires faith, and this step of faith becomes a wedge to break the ice of the oppressive feeling. Whenever I feel I cannot access the love or presence of God, or I cannot lift the weight of a heavy feeling, I get back on the offense with tongues. I speak strongly, loudly, and firmly, and intersperse this with declarations of truth. I continue until I feel a bit of a lift and then I am able to return to a posture of receiving from God. This kind tongues is an offensive weapon. It breaks the grip of my emotions and the oppression of the devil, allowing me to continue exposing and transforming the beliefs of my heart.

Also, because it is part of taking authority, it is important that you speak in an authoritative way. Squeaking out a couple of mousey syllables is not what I'm talking about here. What I'm talking about is something forceful, assertive, and powerful. It has amazed me how this simple practice can transform a person's personality. Many people seem to live on the other side of the wall which tells them to be reserved and mousey, so aggressive tongues breaks the rules. But this is the kind of rule you are supposed to break: rules created by Satan to keep you from being a threat in any way, rules created to keep you from driving him out of your life. If this kind of prayer breaks your social code of ethics, then I would suggest this is all the more reason you need to do it. Rise up and take authority!

DELIVERANCE

Recently we held a conference teaching the material in this book. For several hours we explained all the components of taking responsibility, and the need for total surrender to God. When we had the altar call, many people responded, but one was particularly memorable. She started deep groaning and coughing like someone getting deliverance. This lasted for at least half an hour and then there was a sense of release and freedom. What happened?

What happened was that this woman repented. When she repented, it left no room for the devil, and he came out. We never had to preach on demons. Repentance was enough. This is exactly why we do not place an emphasis on the role of Satan. He is attached to your sin. When you drive sin out of your life, you also drive out Satan.

According to Jesus, demons love to come in and turn your spiritual house into a pig pen (Luke 11:26). If you are deep in sin, you may be a good home for them. Demons are looking for a home in this world where they can sin. They want to push you toward sin, and once you are in it, they want to keep you in it.

154

The farther down the road of sin you go, the more likely you will experience the effects in a personal way. You may hear voices, see manifestations, or feel an unnatural pull toward things more evil than you are naturally interested in. The devil prowls around looking for someone to devour, and if you are having these manifestations, he is trying to devour you.

Some cases require that someone extra help drive a demon out. Usually this is when a person is too oppressed for human reason to be of any real use. These are the kind of people we see Jesus driving demons out of in the Bible. Think of the man who lived in the wilderness and could not be bound even with chains, or the girl who threw herself in the fire. In these types of cases, someone else has to drive the demon out for them, because they cannot drive it out themselves. In cases where a person is oppressed but seeking God, however, it is better if you drive your own demon out. This is because if you do not get it out in the first place, it is unlikely that you will be able to keep it out. Demonic oppression is there because of sin. Getting rid of the devil and your sin are part of the same process.

Let's take a closer look at the problem. Most people talk about "casting out" a demon. The problem with this terminology is that it brings the incorrect idea to mind. "Casting" is the same word used for magic spells, which leads you to think of removing a demon as primarily something you say – like a spell. This is an unfortunate trick of the English language. The underlying Greek word is ἐκβάλλω which literally means to "throw out." This why the NIV authors chose to translate the word as "drive out" instead of "cast out." This creates a very different image doesn't it? "Driving" is what you do to cattle. You get on a horse and force them to go in a certain direction. Satan is removed the same way. He is not going to go when you say *abra cadabra*. He is going to go when you **force** him out. Satan is evil. He is a terrorist. If he can stay, he will. You don't negotiate with him or simply tell him to leave. You force him to leave.

What does it mean to force a demon out? It's not about what you say. It's about what is going on inside. You push out his influence. Every thought, feeling, or experience which is associated with Satan, you force out of your being. You can see why repentance often removes demons – because it involves the same process. A demon is simply a personality associated with a sin pattern.

So only after I have repented and declared my authority in Christ, if I still feel oppressed, do I address the devil. Only after you turn from your sin and reach the point of absolute conviction, can you say "no" to Satan in a way that he must leave. Then you bear down on him and push him out of your being. Every affection, every connection, every negative feeling, everything which chains you to sin must go. You will be free. The enemy encounters your iron-clad faith and absolute resolve, and he cannot stay.

I have had this experience myself and have seen it at work in others. When a real demon is removed there is often a feeling that part of your personality is missing, because his way of thinking was such a part of your life. You may find certain thoughts which you kept thinking just are not there anymore. It's kind of creepy, because you realize that something you thought was you, was really a part of you that had been taken over by something evil. At the same time, there is a sense of great relief because you now have that part of yourself back. After one such session, a man we worked with walked around the house for several days not knowing who he was. He was free from the oppression for the first time in decades. Once you get part of yourself back, make sure to fill it with God!

"Deliverance" is the modern word that has been used for the removal of demons, but the connection I want you to make here is to your authority as a believer. A demon is driven out because you leave sin and your old identity behind and you stand up in your new identity as a son of God. When you drive Satan out in this way, you do not need to fear his return because it was your faith that drove him out, and if he encounters you again, you will do the same. No discussion, no entertaining him, no openness to his ideas, simply ruling over him.

Transformation Takes Time

Perhaps, the biggest reason why people do not get free is that they give up. If you think you are going from zero to hero in five seconds, you've been in too many altar calls. When talking about the Kingdom of God, Jesus consistently uses metaphors involving fruit-bearing plants, such as the wheat and tares, the mustard seed, the fig tree, the vineyard, etc. These metaphors apply to you too. You were made of earth, after all. You are a special creation of God's garden. This is why sowing and reaping applies to you.

Sin involves a process of sowing and reaping. All the sin you have sowed into your body is stored there as emptiness, selfishness, and craving. You may have physical symptoms of withdrawal or you may feel needy. Regardless, it is normal to walk through a period of withdrawal in order to get total victory – it's detox. Visiting these places in your mind's eye, as a surfacing activity, is a first step of exposing and confronting these things. Confronting these moments of craving is the next level of the surfacing process.

As Paul explains in Galatians 6, when you sow to the spirit you reap life, and when you sow to the flesh, you reap death. Just like a garden, however, there is a delayed reaction to sowing and reaping. The life you are experiencing right now is the result of what you have been doing over the course of the last several years. To have a new life, you must start sowing a new harvest. While you are doing that, however, you may continue to reap the harvest of how you were living and thinking for quite some time. It took you a long time to become the way you are, so you should expect it to take time to become more like God.

In fact, the first thing that most people experience when they start down the path of repentance is massive opposition. You feel like you keep hitting brick walls. You're tired, you're guilty, you want to give up. These are all actually good signs. It means you stopped stuffing your sin down into the secret places in your heart and brought it out in the open. You ripped the band-aid off. Not only that, but you stopped medicating the pain of sin with something else. You're doing things without painkillers. It may hurt to face it, but freedom is in your grasp.

It is exactly at this point that a lot of people turn back. The pain of facing sin's fallout is too great so they go back to the old theology they tried before, which allowed them to keep sin in the closet. One man I work with has done this at least a half-dozen times. As soon as he sees himself in the mirror, he runs and goes back to the same old theology that failed him before. Six months later it fails him again, and he gives me a call. Don't give up when you experience pain, or when you see yourself as you really are. Press forward and you will get the victory. These things you are afraid of are the things you have not finished confronting. They are exactly what has kept you from breaking free. Do something different this time.

If pain doesn't make you turn back, many people report that the devil then sweetens the pot with temptation. Often this is an old friend or romantic interest, but it could be anything. One of my friends even had his old drug dealer come to his church and lure him out for a bit of weed. You give into that temptation and then you are back down the road of destruction you were on before. I have something to tell you, though – falling back into sin does not mean the end of the road. In fact, almost no one quits anything cold turkey, the first time.

The difference between people who get ultimately free and people who do not is how they respond if they do fall into sin. It's natural to hate yourself, feel guilty, feel like a failure, and basically want to quit. But you do not have to take this route. If you fall down, dust yourself off, get up, and start running in the right direction again. My friend whose dealer brought him the weed *did* give into temptation that one time and it messed up his life for awhile. But he came to his senses and got out. Now he is an amazing man of God. Don't destroy your freedom over one slip. Take the long view.

As much as you may want it to be, living free of sin is not an event; it is a lifestyle. You live in the world and were born of the world, and so each day is an assault against your place of perfect peace and security with Christ. Garbage comes out of your heart, and more garbage is thrown on you. The victories you win along the way will last as long as you continue to abide in Christ.

Christians love stories about people who had a single event where they broke the power of sin because it shows us that God is real and gives us hope that we can break sin as well. What you need to understand, however, is that this is a self-fulfilling prophecy. Because we like these kinds of stories, these are the ones we invite to be heard in church. Furthermore, because it is more impacting, people tell their story with an emphasis on the event.

As any historian will tell you, however, events do not stand on their own; they are part of a long process. We like to tell the story of Martin Luther nailing his 95 Theses to the door of the Wittenburg church, but God was working on Luther for a decade before that happened. And after the Theses were nailed to the door, Luther spent the remaining decades of his life following through on them. Taking this more complete perspective of freedom helps you to understand what it means to walk with God for the long haul.

I have another secret: it is impossible to be a Christian apart from Christ. When Jesus said, "Apart from me you can do nothing," He meant it (John 15:5). No technique in the world will help you if you do not continue drinking from the well of living water. What does abiding in Christ mean? Abiding in Christ means you maintain a place of connection and love with God where the assaults of sin cannot win. When you feel the craving inside your heart, rather than cover it, ignore it, or feed it, realize it is a moment of danger and turn to the perfect love of God. He will cleanse and remove it. Grow strong in the thoughts and love of God as you turn away from the things of this world.

You can do this in a daily time with God. You can do this through a weekly power encounter. You can grow and encounter Him as you minister to others. You can get the breakthrough in worship, or in the morning, noon, or night. What matters is not the time or place you access God, or even the method. What matters is that you learn to draw life from Him on a consistent basis. You will find that, with a little maintenance, you can learn to stay in a place of perfect fellowship with God.

In fact, you could think of abiding in Christ as the sort of "father of all repentance." Specific sins are simply manifestations of your separation from Christ, the Living Vine, and your love for the things of this world in His place. Learning to abide in Christ is therefore the ultimate goal of all repentance. Abiding means learning to draw your life from Him instead of things here on earth. The more you do this, the more peace you will experience, and the more you will become like Him.

I will be perfectly honest: abiding in Christ is a lot like Peter walking on the water. You can go for great stretches, and then fall back into the abyss. You must continue to abide in Him if you want to continue to walk on the water. They key is learning to do what Paul said, over the long run -- put the deeds of the flesh to death through the power of the Spirit (Rom. 8:13). This is repentance applied to your life and identity over time.

DISCIPLINE DEFENDS YOUR FREEDOM

Many who recognize the importance of heart motives think that externals do not matter at all. This leads them to reject things like external discipline, self-denial, fasting, external appearances, and regularity of any kind. In fact, I used to think this way myself until I lived long enough to see the difference between people who have discipline and people who don't. The Bible says that a man who lacks discipline is like a city without walls (Prov. 25:28).

When God created the heavens and the earth, He separated the light from the darkness, and then he established the sun and the moon to rule over the day and night (Gen 1:18). His establishment of days and seasons are His way of bringing order into chaos. Without self-discipline, you are an easy target for the devil, and your life is ripe for descending into sin. This is because you do not have walls of order in your life to defend you, to ensure that the fundamental parts of your life are in order. You need to establish order in your life in order to govern it, in the same way God established order to the universe.

And if you have been living in sin, your discipline has been destroyed even more, to the point where you may not be able to function at all. This is why people in tough shape often check into a program. Even if the program does nothing directly for your inner life, it helps you do something that is almost impossible to do on your own – reestablish the walls of order and discipline around your life. It prevents you from being ruled by your passions so that you can be ruled by God instead. In fact, for many people whose walls have already been deeply broken down by the ravages of sin and personal passions, discipline can be the only way back.

Discipline is therefore a way of building up your life. It is a way of making sure you have time for God and cannot be sidetracked. It is a way of making sure you can accomplish what needs to be accomplished. It is true that discipline or self-denial, done for the wrong reasons, can make you irritable and even Pharisaical. But discipline for the right reasons is very important.

It is a myth in our generation that only the internals matter, and the externals do not matter at all. Actually they operate in a cycle. External limits set boundaries of behavior which motivate you to make proper heart changes. These heart changes lead you to present proper external fruit. This is quite easy to see when raise children. They will respond exactly to whatever limits you set. If you set no limits, they will act like animals. If you set higher ones, they function well within them. Good outer limits of discipline help shape the inner heart.

Today, we think Jesus was only about the inner life, but in reality He wanted the inner and outer lives to match. This is why He told the disciples to do as the Pharisees said, but not as they did (Mat 23:2). Many of their leadership's outward practices were helpful and desirable, but their heart motivations for doing them were wrong. Therefore, discipline and order are liberating, not stifling. I say all of this because self-discipline is an important part of a successful long term walk with God. I'm not saying you need to be military or anything like that. What I am saying is that self-discipline, when built on top of a heart which is hungry for

God, is helpful. And developing boundaries and order helps solidify the gains you have made in God. If your life is in disorder then it is all too easy to spiral away from God without even knowing it.

HOW FAR CAN I GO IN GOD?

There may be nothing in the world quite as satisfying as being clean again after going down the muddy road of sin. In this final section, we have given you some insight into structures which hold sin in place, how to tear them down, and how to push sin out of your life.

This Freedom Process you have learned is not simply about breaking free of besetting sin, however. God did not save you just to get rid of sin. He saved you to bring you and others into the place of perfect eternal fellowship. There is a depth in God that few Christians even believe exists, and most of those who do cannot figure out how to attain it. They have been stopped because our modern methods have tried to wish sin away instead of confronting and removing it. This book has attempted to clear the cobwebs away and open a door to the deeper life.

If you continue to apply the steps of freedom and abide in Christ, sin will become less and less of an issue, and the heights of God will come more and more in view. Repentance is the process by which you can encounter the living God in deeper and deeper ways. Really there are no limits. Remember my friend who was called up into heaven after he learned the art of repentance? What will God do in your life when you start down the narrow road with Him? Look up into the infinite glory of God. You'll begin to realize you are no longer waiting on God to access the deeper place with Him, but that He is waiting on you. The Father is waiting for you to come up out of this world and enter into the heavenly paradise of being one with Him.

You don't have to go to a conference or hear an exciting story to keep motivated. When you walk with God consistently, your life will become the story. You do not have to wait for a prophecy, a visit from heaven, or some other supernatural encounter in order to move on with God. You now have the tools in your hands to go as deep and as far with God as you want to go. There is no secret to entering in. It is in plain view. With nothing standing between you and the Creator of the universe, all things are truly possible. And as you begin to step into the heavenly realm by faith, you will bring heaven into earth. Christ living in you is the inbreaking of the New Creation.

Cloud, Henry and John Townsend. *It's Not My Fault*. Walton-on-Thames: Thomas Nelson, 2007.

Finney, Charles. *God in You*. Springdale: Whitaker House, 1998.

Finney, Charles. *Living Your Faith*. New York: Whitaker House, 2008.

Liardon, Roberts. Breaking controlling powers. New Kensington, PA: Whitaker House, 2005.

Luther, Martin. Galatians. Wheaton: Crossway Books, 1998.

Marshall, Walter and Bruce H. Mcrae. The Gospel Mystery of Sanctification. City: Wipf & Stock Publishers, 2005.

Osborn, T. L. *The Message That Works*. Tulsa: Osborn Publishers, 2004.

Richards, James. *Breaking the Cycle*. Legacy Publishers International, 2003.

Richards, James. *Escape from Codependent Christianity*. Treasure House, 2003.

Richards, James. *Grace The Power to Change*. New York: Whitaker House, 2001.

Richards, James B. *How to Stop the Pain*. New York: Whitaker House, 2001.